DINING IN-PORTLAND

$7.95

OTHER TITLES IN SERIES:
Dining In—Chicago
Dining In—Dallas
Dining In—Houston
Dining In—Los Angeles
Dining In—Minneapolis/St. Paul
Dining In—Monterey Peninsula
Dining In—Philadelphia
Dining In—Pittsburgh
Dining In—St. Louis
Dining In—San Francisco
Dining In—Seattle
Dining In—Toronto

DINING IN-PORTLAND

A Collection of Gourmet Recipes for Complete Meals
from Portland's Finest Restaurants

By Muriel Bevilacqua Logan and Emily Crumpacker
Foreword by Warren J. Iliff

PEANUT BUTTER PUBLISHING

Peanut Butter Towers   Seattle, Washington 98134

Cover Photography by Dale Windham

Copyright © 1979 by Peanut Butter Publishing
All rights reserved.
Printed in the United States of America
ISBN 0-89716-043-6

First Printing November 1979

Contents

Foreword	*vii*
Belinda's	1
Brasserie Montmartre	13
Couch Street Fish House	21
Crêpe Faire	29
Eat Your Heart Out	35
Genoa	43
Henry Thiele's	53
Huber's	61
Indigine	69
Jake's	75
L'Escargot	83
L'Auberge	91
The London Grill	99
Old Portland Post Office	109
Pettygrove House	119
Señor Korte	127
Silver Garden Restaurant	135
Uncle Chen's	145
Vat and Tonsure	153
Winterborne	161
The Woodstove	171
Index	*183*
About the Authors	*189*

FOREWORD

There are many ways to learn about a city. To know Portland, for instance, you could read about its distinctive neighborhoods—or you could board a boat and discover Portland through its Willamette River bridges. By bicycle you could investigate its parks; by foot you could refresh yourself at the city's many water fountains. While all of these are excellent approaches to our special city, none can rival getting to know it through its restaurants—and DINING IN—PORTLAND is a very special guide to doing so.

This unique book combines the best restaurants with their best recipes and, in so doing, combines two of Portland's culinary claims to fame. On the one hand we have 21 superb restaurants with a gourmet's suggestions for an ideal menu and an ideal evening of dining. And on the other, we can follow in the tradition of fine cooking begun by Portland's James Beard and his associate Richard Nelson, continuing now with a new generation of chefs that has been trained by my wife's good friend, Anne Willan, the owner and *directrice* of Paris' highly respected Ecole de Cuisine La Varenne.

Emily Crumpacker, another of Portland's own, is a graduate of that school and is herself now an instructor of fine cooking (beginning at L'Academie Paris-Americaine before returning to the States to instruct at La Cuisine School of Cooking in Seattle). Her co-author, Muriel Logan, divides her time between traveling, attending cooking schools in France and in Seattle, writing for gourmet publications...and becoming the first woman apprentice in one of Seattle's finest restaurant kitchens!

Emily and Muriel have done a superb job with descriptions, instructions and restaurant selections, with the result that my wife and I look forward to taking on the challenges of the menus included—and, of course, tasting the finished products!

> Warren J. Iliff,
> Director of Washington Park Zoo

Belinda's

Dinner for Four

Chilled Oregon Crawfish
Sauce Remoulade

Purée of Parsnip Soup

Sweetbreads Meunière

Veal Chops aux Fines Herbes

Greens with Fresh Basil Dressing

Fresh Raspberry Tart

Wines:

With Crawfish—Henry-Hinsdale Chalone Chardonnay, '77
With Sweetbreads—Château Laville Haut Brion Graves, '75
With Veal—Château Ducru Beaucaillon, St. Julien, '70
With Tart—Château Suduirant Sauternes, '62

Ross Pullen, Owner & Chef

Dining at Belinda's, a charming small restaurant in the quiet southeast neighborhood of Sellwood, is a pleasant experience that mirrors the values of owner-chef Ross Pullen. Many Portland diners who have made Belinda's a favorite since its opening in 1977 express a desire to keep this little spot their own secret.

Pullen, a man who believes in great attention to detail, feels that by limiting the size and scope of his operation he has the key to creating the pleasant, stable atmosphere he seeks. Dreaming of having his own restaurant while he worked as cook and manager in Marin County in California and Boise, Idaho, Pullen developed a deeply-held philosophy: establishing security and permanence in his employees would, in return, foster such feelings in customers—that this restaurant was "a good place to be". One example of the way Pullen's life is very much tied up in his restaurant family ("without good employees you don't have anything") is how the entire Belinda's staff sits down to dinner together at 4:30 every afternoon before settling into the evening rush.

With two young assistants in the kitchen "prepping" and baking, Ross prepares all the entrées to order himself. In the interests of variety and creativity, Belinda's substantial menu is changed every few months. His wine list, which he intends to make "one of the best in the Pacific Northwest", is changed every four or five weeks to reflect his actual cellar. An example of his acumen and ability to serve his patrons well: Chardonnays currently being in such short supply, he acquired all the good Chardonays he could—37 at present—for a special wine list.

8324 SE 17th

*I would like to present recipes that people read and are afraid of but, when they look at how to do them, aren't afraid anymore —
I'd like to get rid of some of the myths and show people how easy these things can be.*

Chilled Oregon Crawfish

36 fresh live Oregon crawfish, washed
Spiced Court Bouillon
Romaine leaves
Garnish: lemon wedges
       parsley
Sauce Remoulade

1. Remove small wing in center of tail of each crawfish before adding to simmering court bouillon. Cook 5 minutes.
2. Remove pot from heat and cool crawfish in liquid at least 2 hours.
3. Drain well and arrange on bed of romaine on large platter. Garnish with lemon wedges and parsley. Serve **Sauce Rémoulade** on the side. Supply picks and crackers and lots of napkins.

SPICED COURT BOUILLON

1 gallon water
1 gallon dry white wine
Pickling spice to taste
6 cloves garlic, peeled
2 cinnamon sticks
2 small onions, peeled and stuck with cloves, leaving tops intact
    to keep them from falling apart
Salt and freshly ground pepper to taste

Combine all ingredients. Bring to a boil and simmer 20 minutes.

SAUCE REMOULADE

1 pint good quality mayonnaise, preferably homemade
2 hard-cooked eggs, chopped
¼ cup chopped cornichons (imported sour gherkin pickles)
2 cloves garlic, finely minced
2 tablespoons finely minced onions
1 tablespoon finely minced parsley
1 tablespoon finely minced fresh tarragon
1 tablespoon finely minced fresh chervil
1 teaspoon Dijon mustard
1 tablespoon red wine vineger, preferably imported or Four Monks
2 flat anchovies, mashed
1 tablespoon chopped capers

Combine all ingredients. Let stand at least 2 hours before serving.

TIP: If fresh herbs are not available use ¼ amount of dried product.

Purée of Parsnip Soup

1 bay leaf
1 teaspoon dried marjoram
½ teaspoon dried chervil
¼ teaspoon dried whole thyme
1 pound butter
6 parsnips, scrubbed clean and chopped
3 carrots, scrubbed and chopped
1 medium onion, peeled and chopped
2 cloves garlic, finely minced
2 tablespoons chopped fresh parsley
2 quarts chicken stock, preferably homemade
Salt and white pepper to taste

1. Grind dry herbs together until very fine.
2. Melt ¾ pound butter in a large, heavy skillet over medium heat. Add vegetables and sauté 5 to 10 minutes. Add dried herbs and parsley and continue cooking, stirring often. Add more butter if necessary and cook until vegetables are tender and golden brown, being careful not to burn them.
3. Purée vegetables in food processor or blender until completely smooth.
4. Meanwhile, bring chicken stock to simmer. Add purée mixture and simmer 15 to 20 minutes. Add salt and pepper and correct seasoning.
5. Using whip, mix in remaining ¼ pound butter and serve.

TIP: This soup may be made ahead and reheated. If so, add final ¼ pound butter just before serving.

We look for ideas for dishes that maybe aren't so unique, so kooky, but that are consistently good. I like to impress with the taste of foods more than with the visual factor. I want people to say, "Oh! How fresh it is!" rather than create a visual shock effect..."

Sweetbreads Meuniere

1 to 1½ pounds veal sweetbreads
Court Bouillon
Vegetable oil
Flour
Salt and freshly ground pepper
⅛ pound butter
1 tablespoon finely minced shallot
¼ cup chopped fresh parsley
½ lemon
Garnish: 12 lemon wedges

1. Place sweetbreads in cold water for several hours or overnight. If there are any blood clots, change water often.
2. Poach sweetbreads in **Court Bouillon** 8 to 10 minutes or until they just start to firm. Remove from heat and add ice to stop cooking process. Chill in liquid.
3. Remove from liquid and pull off any fat or membrane between glands. Dry on towel and slice about ¼" thick; dry again.
4. Heat oil to cover in sauté pan large enough to hold all slices easily.
5. Dust slices in flour seasoned with salt and pepper. Shake off excess flour and brown both sides in oil over medium heat until golden brown, about 2 to 5 minutes each side. Set aside on paper towels.
6. Wipe pan clean and add sweetbreads again. Add butter and cook over high heat until butter is thoroughly melted. Add shallots and shake pan often. When shallots start to turn golden, add parsley. Continue shaking until butter is golden brown but do not let it get too dark!
7. Squeeze lemon into pan, holding back pips. Serve sweetbreads immediately in ramekins garnished with lemon wedges.

COURT BOUILLON

3 quarts *cold* water
1 carrot, scrubbed and sliced
1 leek, cleaned and split lengthwise
1 large sprig parsley
1 sprig celery leaf
½ fresh lemon
3 tablespoons salt
1 teaspoon whole peppercorns
1 small onion, peeled and stuck with cloves

Combine all ingredients, squeezing juice from lemon, then adding the half to the pot.

When buying sweetbreads, ask for the round or pancreas gland.

Veal Chops aux Fines Herbes

8 4- to 5-ounce milk fed veal loin chops
Flour for dusting
Salt and freshly ground pepper
2 tablespoons peanut oil, or more if needed
4 tablespoons cold butter, or more if needed
1 tablespoon finely chopped shallots
6 ounces dry white wine
14 ounces brown sauce
¼ cup chopped fresh parsley
1 tablespoon finely chopped fresh chervil, or ½ teaspoon dried
1 tablespoon finely chopped fresh tarragon, or ½ teaspoon dried
Juice of ⅛ lemon

1. Preheat oven to 450 degrees.
2. Dust chops in flour seasoned with salt and pepper.
3. Heat oil and 2 tablespoons butter each in 2 large heavy skillets. Brown chops on both sides adding more oil and butter in equal proportions if needed. Cover pans and place in oven. Cook approximately 8 to 10 minutes or until juices run clear; do not overcook.
4. Remove pans from oven and return to medium high heat. Remove chops to heated platter and keep warm.
5. Pour off excess fat in pan and stir in shallots while scraping up brown bits on bottom of pans over high heat, being careful not to let it burn. Deglaze pans with white wine and combine contents in 1 pan. Boil vigorously until wine is reduced to syrup.
6. Add brown sauce, parsley, chervil and tarragon. Continue boiling. Add juices that have drained from chops. Reduce sauce by ½, shaking pan often.
7. Place chops on hot plates. When sauce is reduced, swirl in remaining 2 tablespoons butter until melted and add lemon juice. Pour over chops. May be served with buttered noodles and your favorite fresh vegetables.

Have butcher trim chops nicely and use a good white wine.

Greens with Fresh Basil Dressing

Salad greens of your choice, especially spinach, romaine, butter lettuce, or red leaf, washed, dried and chilled
Fresh Basil Dressing

Toss chosen greens with dressing and serve immediately on chilled salad plates.

FRESH BASIL DRESSING

½ cup imported red wine vinegar
1 tablespoon water
2 tablespoons sugar
1 tablespoon salt
1 teaspoon freshly ground pepper
2 tablespoons freshly squeezed lemon juice
½ teaspoon Worcestershire
3 tablespoons finely minced shallots
1 tablespoon finely minced garlic
3 tablespoons finely minced fresh parsley
¼ cup finely minced fresh basil, or ⅛ amount dried basil
1½ cups soybean oil or any good quality vegetable oil

1. Combine all ingredients except oil thoroughly.
2. Using whip, beat in oil in a stream until dressing is creamy.

We get Oregon veal and chickens, the best commercial ducks from Michigan, fresh local sturgeon, mussels, and sand dabs, and fresh chanterelles from Mount Hood in the fall.

Fresh Raspberry Tart

1 10" tart shell of **Pâte Brisée**
Crème Patissière à la Liqueur de Framboise
1 pint fresh raspberries
Whipped Cream with Raspberry Liqueur

1. Spread cooled tart shell with **Crème Patissière.**
2. Place raspberries side by side completely filling tart.
3. Pipe rosettes of **Whipped Cream with Raspberry Liqueur** around edges of tart and serve.

PATE BRISEE

1 cup sifted all purpose flour
¼ teaspoon salt
¼ cup butter
1½ tablespoons vegetable shortening
2½ to 3 tablespoons cold water
Beans or rice to weight

1. Preheat oven to 425 degrees.
2. Stir flour and salt in bowl. Add butter and shortening and cut in until mixture resembles coarse meal.
3. Add water and blend quickly using a tossing motion. Press into a ball.
4. Roll into a circle ⅛" thick and 2" larger than the pan. Roll dough over pin and transfer to pan, unrolling carefully. Fit loosely into pan without stretching or breaking dough.
5. Trim edge ½" larger than pan and flute edges. Prick bottom and sides with fork.
6. Line pastry carefully with foil and fill with beans or rice to weight.
7. Bake 10 minutes and remove foil and beans or rice. Bake 2 to 5 minutes more or until shell is golden brown.
8. Cool on rack.

CREME PATISSIERE A LA LIQUEUR DE FRAMBOISE

½ cup sugar
4 tablespoons cornstarch
Pinch salt
2 cups milk
4 large egg yolks
1 tablespoon raspberry liqueur
Butter

1. Combine sugar, cornstarch, and salt in 1½-quart stainless steel or enamel saucepan. Add ¼ cup milk and mix well over low heat.
2. Heat 1½ cups milk and gradually pour into mixture in saucepan, stirring constantly. Stir and cook over medium heat until very thick. Set aside.
3. Beat egg yolks. Blend with remaining ¼ cup milk and add to cooked mixture. Cook over hot water or very low heat, stirring constantly, until cream is thick like mayonnaise.
4. Remove from heat and stir in raspberry liqueur. Dot with butter to prevent crust forming and cool thoroughly. Makes 2 cups.

WHIPPED CREAM WITH RASPBERRY LIQUEUR

4 ounces heavy whipping cream
1 tablespoon sugar
1 tablespoon raspberry liqueur

1. Chill bowl and beaters. Have ready a pastry bag with star tip.
2. Place all ingredients in chilled bowl and beat at high speed until peaks form.
3. Spoon into pastry bag and chill until needed.

TIP: The tart may be made 2 hours ahead and garnished with whipped cream just before serving.

It's an unorthodox life working nights, weekends, and holidays, but I never stand in lines and never get in traffic jams. I hate those things.

BRASSERIE MONTMARTRE
FRENCH RESTAURANT

Dinner for Four

Escargots Bourguignonne

Carre d'Agneau Montmartre

Salade et Brie

Tarte au Citron

Wines:
Aperitif—Kir
With Entrée—Château de Pez

Roger and Sherrie Lextrait, Owners
Roger Lextrait, Head Chef

When Roger and Sherrie Lextrait sold L'Odeon in Lake Oswego several years ago, they took a vacation to France and Mexico. Although they planned to begin business again in another locality when they returned to the States, Portland prevailed; the Lextraits opened the Brasserie Montmartre in late 1978.

There's a dramatic contrast between the street outside and the interior of their large restaurant. High ceilings, black and white marble floors, silk lamps...even Greek columns. Evocations of Paris are enhanced by Edith Piaf recordings during noontime dining; most evenings the diners are entertained by live music.

626 SW Park

Escargots Bourguignonne

1 cup soft butter
8 cloves garlic, pressed
2 tablespoons chopped shallot
2 tablespoons chopped parsley
Pinch nutmeg
24 snails with shells

1. Combine butter, garlic, shallots, parsley and nutmeg thoroughly.
2. In each snail shell put a small amount of butter, then the snail, finishing with more butter mixture.
3. Heat filled shells in a warm oven and serve with French bread.

Carre d'Agneau Montmartre

2 small racks of lamb, 6 chops each
3 tablespoons butter
1 cup breadcrumbs
½ teaspoon ground cumin
½ teaspoon whole tarragon leaves
½ teaspoon whole fennel seeds
½ teaspoon dried chives

1. Preheat oven to 425 degrees.
2. Dot lamb racks with butter.
3. Combine breadcrumbs and spices. Sprinkle over buttered lamb racks.
4. Bake in preheated oven 20 to 30 minutes.
5. Serve with **Rice**, **Carrots** and **Curry Sauce.**

The lamb should be pink when served, with the bone ends well charred.

Rice

½ cup chopped onions
½ cup chopped green peppers
3 tablespoons butter
3 cups water
1½ cups rice

1. Preheat oven to 425 degrees.
2. Sauté onions and peppers in butter.
3. Stir in water and rice. Bake in preheated oven 20 minutes.

Carrots

1½ pounds carrots, peeled and cut julienne
4 tablespoons butter
1 clove garlic, pressed

1. Parboil carrots in large pan of water.
2. Lift out and rinse with cool water.
3. Combine butter and garlic in a pan; add carrots and sauté.

Curry Sauce

½ cup finely chopped onion
½ cup finely chopped green pepper
3 tablespoons butter
1 clove garlic, pressed
1 cup cubed green apples
1½ cups beef stock
1 cup white wine
Roux made with 2 tablespoons melted butter and
   3 tablespoons flour

1. Sauté chopped onion and green pepper in butter.
2. Add garlic, apples and curry powder.
3. Combine stock and wine in a saucepan and reduce by half.
4. Thicken reduction with roux; add vegetable mixture.
5. Bring to a boil, lower heat and simmer 20 minutes.

Salade et Brie

1 part vinegar to 3 parts oil
Salt and pepper
Fresh greens, washed and well dried
Wedge of Brie cheese

1. Combine vinegar, oil, salt and pepper.
2. Pour over greens, and toss.
3. Serve on individual salad plates with a wedge of Brie on the side.

Tarte au Citron

SWEET DOUGH

1¼ cups flour
¼ cup sugar
6 tablespoons butter
3 tablespoons margarine
1 egg yolk
3 tablespoons water

1. Preheat oven to 375 degrees.
2. Toss flour and sugar together in a bowl.
3. Add butter, margarine and egg yolk. Work ingredients together with fingertips.
4. Add water and work until smooth.
5. Roll out dough; line an 8" tart mold.
6. Bake 10 minutes in preheated oven. Set aside.

LEMON FILLING

¼ cup butter
1 cup sugar
4 eggs
3 tablespoons cream
¼ cup lemon juice
¼ cup orange juice
Apricot jam
Grated coconut
Garnish: orange slices

1. Combine butter and sugar until smooth. Add eggs 1 at a time, beating thoroughly after each addition.
2. Mix in cream; add juices.
3. Pour mixture into partially baked tart shell; bake at 375 degrees 20 minutes, or until set. Let cool.
4. Paint border with apricot jam and apply grated coconut along the edge.
5. Garnish with orange slices.

Dinner for Four

Ceviche

Sorrel and Oyster Soup

Watercress, Butter Lettuce and Shrimp Salad

Red and White

Tomatoes Stuffed with Cauliflower Purée

Chocolate Fondue

Wines:
With Ceviche, Salad and Soup—Château Laville-Haut-Brion, '76
With Salmon—Corton Charlemagne, '74 or '75
With Fondue—Serriger Vogelsang Eiswein, '75

Horst Mäger and Bob Williamson, Owners
Marcel Lahsenne, Chef

Coming to the United States at twenty-one from Wiesbaden, Horst Mäger couldn't speak English but had training and experience as a chef—the sixth chef in his family. Undeterred by the language barrier, Mäger soon established himself in the culinary community as an innovator, presenting Portland with its beloved German restaurant, the Rheinlander. With his partner, Bob Williamson, he continues his introduction of new ideas and cuisines to the city. The Couch Street Fish House, Mäger's third specialty restaurant, represented a new phenomenon for Portland diners at its opening in 1976: an elegant, sophisticated, small seafood house offering specialties from around the world as well as from local sources.

The restaurant's interior is decorated with a tasteful combination of old and new: antique furnishings combined with modern paintings and metal sculptures, exposed brick walls contrasted with elegant upholstered banquettes, and tanks showcasing live local trout, Maine lobsters and other fresh *fruits de mer*. The diner is seated with a flair: each napkin holds a long-stemmed carnation, and a huge silver tray displaying a selection of seafood hors d'oeuvres—ranging from ceviche to salmon mousse—is offered for the diner's enjoyment while perusing the menu, which features such local delectables as Columbia River caviar, perch and salmon, as well as Dover sole and occasionally mahi mahi, swordfish and abalone.

The preparations showcase the chefs' skills at preparing a wide range of possibilities, from the simplest *meunière* to elaborate *sole Waleska*.

A basic Mäger principal is to hire the best qualified personnel. "It's just too expensive to hire cheap help. The quality of my restaurant depends upon the workers; if I get dynamite help I have a dynamite restaurant." Chef Marcel Lahsenne studied at the Culinary Institute of America in New York. He and other staff members are serious young professionals with high standards. "Our customers expect a great deal, and we strive to deliver. The day we stop trying to improve is the day we quit the business."

105 NW 3rd Avenue

Ceviche

½ pound scallops, cut in ½" cubes
½ yellow onion, diced small
2 jalapeño peppers, seeded, diced small
1 red pepper, seeded, diced small
Juice of 8 limes
Juice of ½ lemon
Salt and freshly ground pepper to taste
Garnish: 4 tomato wedges

1. Combine all ingredients in a clay bowl.
2. Toss gently and allow to marinate at least 2 hours.
3. Serve in 4 cocktail glasses with tomato wedges for garnish.

Watercress, Butter Lettuce and Shrimp Salad

2 heads butter lettuce
1 bunch watercress
5 ounces vinaigrette dressing
Garnish: 5 ounces bay shrimp meat
              4 slices lemon

1. Arrange outer leaves of butter lettuce around sides and bottom of a bowl.
2. Break the hearts of lettuce into small pieces by hand and toss with watercress and vinaigrette.
3. Put tossed lettuce into lined bowl; garnish with bay shrimp and lemon slices.

We are in the entertainment business—we entertain the customer with food and service. The customer is our best critic.

Sorrel and Oyster Soup

1 teaspoon minced onion
1 teaspoon butter
8 medium oysters, shucked
¼ cup Chablis
Juice of ½ small lemon
2 bunches fresh sorrel
3 egg yolks
2 cups half-and-half
Salt and pepper as desired
Garnish: 1 cup whipped cream

1. In a skillet sauté onion in butter until almost transparent.
2. Add oysters and sauté briefly.
3. Add Chablis and lemon juice; cook only until edges of oysters curl.
4. Remove oysters to a platter. Add sorrel to skillet and simmer until fully wilted.
5. Combine oysters, sorrel, egg yolks, and 1 cup of half-and-half in blender until smooth.
6. Bring remaining half-and-half to a boil. Add purée.
7. Heat soup almost to a boil, stirring constantly—the egg yolks should thicken it considerably. Check seasoning, adding salt and pepper if needed.
8. Ladle soup into ovenproof bowls, top with whipped cream, and glaze each bowl under the broiler to a light brown.

Red and White

1 pound halibut
1 egg white
¼ cup cream
¾ pound salmon
4 tablespoons butter
2 cups white wine
12 mushroom caps
2 tablespoons flour
Salt and pepper to taste
Garnish: ½ cup whipped cream
Small new red potatoes, boiled
Fresh green beans, boiled or steamed
Tomatoes Stuffed with Cauliflower Purée

1. Purée 4 ounces halibut with egg white. Beat until smooth and light.
2. Slowly beat in cream. Chill this mousse-like mixture until thoroughly cool.
3. Slice remaining halibut and salmon into 4 thin slices each. Spread each halibut slice with ¼ of the mousse. Place salmon slices on top and press firmly to bind together.
4. Butter bottom of a pan large enough to hold 4 portions with 2 tablespoons butter. Add wine and mushrooms and poach gently until fish is partly cooked. Remove from heat.
5. In saucepan melt remaining butter; add flour. Cook roux over low heat about 4 minutes. Do not brown.
6. Add wine in which fish poached, stirring to make a smooth sauce. Salt and pepper to taste. Cook over low heat 5 minutes. Cool just slightly.
7. Stir whipped cream into warm—not hot—sauce.
8. Place 3 mushroom caps on top of each portion of fish. Coat with sauce.
9. Serve with new red potatoes, fresh green beans, and **Tomatoes Stuffed with Cauliflower Purée**.

TOMATOES STUFFED WITH CAULIFLOWER PUREE

4 firm, ripe tomatoes
Salt
1 small head cauliflower
Butter
Salt and pepper
Cream—optional

1. Stem tomatoes and hollow out space for stuffing. Salt openings and invert on rack to drain 15 minutes.
2. Break cauliflower into flowerets and steam until very tender. Purée through food mill or in blender or food processor. Season with butter, salt and pepper. Stir in a little cream if desired.
3. Preheat oven to 350 degrees.
4. Fill tomato cases with cauliflower purée. Place in a pan with enough water to prevent scorching or in well-greased muffin tins. Bake 10 to 15 minutes or until heated through but not too soft.

Chocolate Fondue

1 apple, cored and sliced
Juice of ½ lemon—optional
2 bananas, peeled and sliced
8 strawberries
6 ounces semi-sweet chocolate
1 ounce Kirschwasser
12 marshmallows

1. Prepare all fruit and arrange on platter. Lemon juice may be squeezed over to prevent discoloration.
2. Melt chocolate very gently in double boiler.
3. Pour chocolate into a small fondue pot and keep warm over a candle flame.
4. Pour Kirschwasser onto chocolate and flame with a match.
5. Use long skewers or fondue forks, toast marshmallows and then dip fruit in chocolate.

Dinner for Six

Marinated Dungeness Crab Salad

Gâteau of Puréed Vegetables and Chicken Mousseline
with Mustard Sauce

Raspberry Ice

Beverages:

With Crab Salad—Domaine Chandon Blanc de Noir
With Gâteau—Erath Chardonnay
With Raspberry Ice—French Press Coffee and
Sandeman Vintage Port, '62

Hank and Helen Hazen, Owners & Chefs

The idea of a crêperie first came to Hank and Helen Hazen during a bicycle trip through Europe. When Portland's Old Town was just beginning its face lift in 1974, the couple opened their Crêpe Faire. Right from that beginning, their purpose was to develop a simple, comfortable restaurant with a European flair. Helen assumed organization of the kitchen, while Hank took on furniture-building and the business management.

There is a friendly and casual feeling to the restaurant which seats about fifty inside; during sunny months, the Crêpe Faire offers lunch served at sidewalk tables under an awning. Specials change regularly, with crêpes being offered in both sweet and savory dishes.

117 NW 2nd Avenue

Marinated Dungeness Crab Salad

½ cup olive oil
6 tablespoons white wine vinegar
2½ teaspoons salt
1½ teaspoons freshly ground pepper
½ teaspoon dry English mustard
⅛ teaspoon thyme
1 tablespoon minced fresh basil
2 tablespoons minced fresh parsley
2½ cups minced green onions
¼ teaspoon sugar
4 tablespoons lime juice
2 pounds fresh Dungeness crabmeat
Garnish: cucumber
 tomato
 hard-cooked egg

1. Combine all ingredients *except* crabmeat and garnishes, and mix together thoroughly for the marinade.
2. Add crabmeat and toss carefully to distribute the marinade.
3. Refrigerate 3 to 4 hours and serve well chilled on soft lettuce leaves, garnished with slices of cucumber, tomato and hard-cooked egg.

Gâteau of Puréed Vegetables and Chicken Mousseline

3 heads cauliflower
2 pounds green beans
2 pounds carrots
3 eggs
1 cup fresh breadcrumbs
Salt and pepper, to taste
1½ pounds boneless, skinless chicken breasts
½ cup cream
9 7" Crêpes
Mustard Sauce

1. Cook vegetables separately in boiling salted water until tender. Refresh in cold water.
2. Purée each vegetable separately in the food grinder and press through a fine sieve.
3. Place each purée in a separate saucepan and cook slowly to evaporate excess moisture.
4. Add 1 egg, well-beaten, to each purée and enough breadcrumbs until each mixture holds a shape.
5. Season carefully with salt and pepper.
6. In a food processor, grind the uncooked chicken breasts until very fine.
7. Add cream, seasoning with salt and pepper to taste.
8. Preheat oven to 350 degrees.
9. Butter a straight-sided 7" to 8" diameter mold and line with parchment paper.
10. Place first crêpe, brown side down, on bottom of mold. Spread with half of chicken mixture on top; cover with another crêpe, brown side down.
11. Spread with half of carrot purée, add another crêpe, spread with half of cauliflower purée, another crêpe and half the bean purée.
12. Repeat process, topping "gâteau" with a final crêpe.
13. Bake in a water bath about 30 minutes or until firm.
14. Invert onto a serving platter. Serve individual wedges surrounded by **Mustard Sauce.**

CREPES

3 eggs
1½ cups milk
Scant cup flour
1 teaspoon sugar

1. Place all ingredients in a blender or food processor and blend together.
2. Cover batter; let it rest overnight in the refrigerator.
3. When ready to fry crêpes, butter crêpe pan lightly. Stir batter and, with a ladle, place a thin coating of batter in crêpe pan.
4. Remove from pan when bottom of crêpe is brown and a little crispy.

MUSTARD SAUCE

2 shallots, chopped
2 tablespoons butter
¼ cup Cognac
1 cup chicken stock
1 cup cream
Squeeze of lemon juice
2 tablespoons Dijon mustard

1. Sauté chopped shallots in 1 tablespoon butter for 1 minute.
2. Add Cognac and reduce by half.
3. Add chicken stock and cream; reduce to a thick golden cream.
4. Stir in lemon juice and mustard.
5. Add remaining butter to sauce and stir until well blended.

Raspberry Ice

1 cup sugar
2 cups water
4 pints fresh raspberries
2 tablespoons fresh lemon juice

1. Bring sugar and water to a boil in a saucepan for 5 minutes.
2. Remove from heat and let syrup cool.
3. Purée raspberries through a food mill or sieve.
4. Combine cooled syrup with raspberry purée.
5. Add lemon juice.
6. Freeze in a covered container, stirring 3 or 4 times, until frozen.
7. Scrape frozen ice with a heavy scoop; fill champagne glasses.

The ice has a coarse texture. It's pretty when garnished with a sprig of mint and a thin, sweet wafer.

Dinner for Four

Chilled Cucumber Soup

Morrocain Salad

Middle East Casserole

Lemon Mousse with Fresh Raspberry Sauce

Monica Grinnell and Marilyn Sloan, Owners

Eat Your Heart Out is the invention and design of Monica Grinnell and Marilyn Sloan, proprietors of a successful catering service of the same name. The restaurant and catering service share the same open kitchen. Hearts everywhere greet the customer upon entering, reflecting the entire feeling of both management and clientele.

"We try to introduce people to new experiences in foods, and because of the exposed kitchen, the chefs are in constant contact with the diners, often discussing recipes and new suggestions for the menu," says Monica. "It is a seasonal kitchen, a way of life," adds Marilyn, "with availability of foods dictating the menu."

"Our food is an extension of ourselves. We are constantly changing, exploring. Just as we insist on originality and client personality in our catering, we put something new into each restaurant day."

"We are a fortunate team. We have worked and grown together for five years, with husbands and children the backbone of our growth. Hundreds of old and new friends each year let us know that they are 'simpatico' with our attitudes—quality, creativity and enjoyment! From the simplest to the most sophisticated taste, everything is cooked with the same love."

831 NW 23rd

Chilled Cucumber Soup

2 English cucumbers
2 lemon cucumbers
4 cups chicken broth
1 onion, minced
4 scallions, minced
3 tablespoons minced parsley
2 cups cream
Salt and pepper

1. Peel, seed and dice cucumbers, reserving some for garnish.
2. Combine cucumbers, broth, onion, scallions, and parsley in a saucepan; cook until cucumbers and onions are soft, stirring occasionally.
3. Purée mixture in batches in the blender. Stir in cream. Season to taste with salt and pepper, and chill.
4. Garnish with reserved chopped cucumber and chives.

TIP: Use equivalent amount of standard cucumbers if the English and lemon are not available. Since English cucumbers are 1½ to 2 times the size of regular, and lemon are much shorter, four or five standard should do.

Middle East Casserole

2 medium eggplants, skinned
1 pound lamb, cut into small cubes
3 tablespoons olive oil
3 cloves garlic, minced
1½ cups minced onion
2 cups brown rice
1 cup chopped walnuts
2 tomatoes, peeled, seeded, and chopped
½ cup breadcrumbs
1 cup grated Cheddar cheese
½ cup grated Parmesan cheese
½ cup chicken broth
1½ tablespoons curry powder
Salt and pepper to taste
1½ cups raisins
15 sheets phyllo dough
Melted butter

1. Cut skinned eggplant into ½" cubes.
2. Sauté in lightly oiled skillet 2 layers at a time. Replenish oil as needed.
3. In another skillet, sauté lamb cubes until brown and cooked through. Transfer to large bowl.
4. Heat olive oil; add garlic and onion and sauté until softened. Add eggplant and onion mixtures to lamb. Set aside to cool.
5. Add rice, walnuts, tomatoes, breadcrumbs, cheeses, chicken broth, curry powder, salt, pepper and raisins. Combine mixture well.
6. In a 9"×12" casserole, layer 5 sheets of phyllo dough, brushing each sheet with melted butter.
7. Add half the lamb mixture, 5 more sheets phyllo dough (again brushing each with melted butter), and remainder of lamb mixture. Top with remaining 5 sheets of phyllo brushed with melted butter.
8. Bake at 350 degrees 45 minutes to 1 hour.

Serve with plain yogurt and chutney as garnishes.

Morrocain Salad

4 tomatoes, peeled, seeded and chopped
2 green peppers, seeded and chopped
Vinaigrette with Cumin

Combine tomatoes and peppers. Toss gently with **Vinaigrette with Cumin.**

VINAIGRETTE WITH CUMIN

1 teaspoon salt
2 tablespoons white wine vinegar
1 clove garlic, mashed
8 tablespoons olive oil
1 tablespoon ground cumin

Combine all ingredients well.

Lemon Mousse with Fresh Raspberry Sauce

½ cup sugar
4 eggs, separated
Juice of 2 medium lemons
1 cup heavy cream, whipped
Grated rind from 2 lemons
Fresh Raspberry Sauce

1. In the top of a double boiler beat egg yolks with sugar until mixture is a light lemon color.
2. Add lemon juice and cook over simmering water, whisking constantly, until mixture heavily coats the spoon. *Do not boil.* Cool mixture.
3. Beat egg whites until stiff; gently fold into lemon mixture.
4. Fold in whipped cream and lemon rind. Place in 4 individual dessert dishes. Just before serving, top with **Fresh Raspberry Sauce.**

FRESH RASPBERRY SAUCE

1½ cups raspberries, gently mashed
1½ tablespoons Grand Marnier
1 to 2 teaspoons powdered sugar

Combine above ingredients.

Dinner for Six

Bagna Cauda

Minestrone Verde al Pesto

Fettuccine alla Carbonara

Branzino alla Zoni

Filleta alla Cacciatore

Carote al Burro e Formaggio

Patate Arrosto

Boccone Dolce

Wines:

With Bagna—Punt e Mes
With Fettuccine—Gattinara
or
Ridge Fiddletown, Zinfandel, '74
With Branzino—Lugana
or
The Eyrie, Chardonnay, '76
With Filleta—Brunello di Montalcino, '70
or
Heitz Cellars "Martha's Vineyard,"
Cabernet Sauvignon, '69
With Boccone Dolce—Asti Spumanti
or
Domaine Chandon, Brut

Chris Rocca and Grey Wolfe, Owners

A new dimension has been added to Portland dining by the format at the Genoa, a quiet and comfortable restaurant specializing in Northern Italian fare. The fixed-price menu of seven-course meals—which changes every two weeks—is recited to the diner, complete with explanations of the various courses. Generally, the menu consists of an appetizer, soup, pasta, choice of three entrées, vegetable and choice of dessert. (The menu's flexibility allows for variance between six and seven course meals, depending upon the chef's creative choices.) Monday is international vegetarian night at the Genoa, again multiple-course but with meat eliminated.

The unique menus and their presentation were planned and executed by owners Chris Rocca and his wife Grey Wolfe, who took over ownership of the restaurant in 1975, although Rocca has been involved with the Genoa since its inception in 1971.

2832 SE Belmont

Bagna Cauda

2 cups heavy cream
2 cloves garlic
2½-ounce can flat anchovies, drained of oil
Dash cayenne
¼ cup unsalted butter

1. In heavy saucepan, simmer cream with 2 garlic cloves until reduced to 1 cup.
2. Place reduced cream, anchovies and cayenne in blender and purée.
3. Bring sauce to a simmer and add butter, stirring until melted.
4. Serve in a hot chafing dish accompanied with chilled, raw vegetables and homemade (if possible) sourdough *grissini*.

TIP: If butter and cream separate, pour in a bit of cold cream and whisk hard. The sauce will regain its velvety texture.

This is a dish to be enjoyed without ceremony. Pick up vegetables or breadsticks—grissini—with your fingers and dip into the sauce until well covered; consume.

Minestrone Verde al Pesto

SOUP:

1½ cups sliced onions
3 tablespoons olive oil
2 cups shelled lima beans, fresh or frozen
6 cups boiling water
1 teaspoon salt
1 cup shelled green peas, fresh or frozen
2 pounds fresh spinach or 2 10-ounce packages thawed frozen spinach

1. Sauté onions in olive oil until tender, about 10 minutes.
2. Add lima beans to boiling salted water and boil uncovered; just before they are tender, add peas and spinach so that all 3 finish cooking together.
3. Add onions to soup and continue cooking for another minute. Purée.
4. Stir a cupful into **Pesto** by driblets. Add remainder by ladlefuls, stirring continually.

*You may serve the **Soup** and **Pesto** separately and allow each person to blend to his own taste.*

PESTO:

1 strip blanched bacon, minced
2 cloves garlic
12 fresh basil leaves
3 tablespoons fresh parsley
2 egg yolks
½ cup grated Parmesan cheese
⅓ cup olive oil

1. Process bacon, garlic, basil, parsley, egg yolks and cheese in food processor until you have a thick mass.
2. Add oil by droplets.

You may do all of this by hand using a mortar and pestle for which pesto is named.

Fettuccine alla Carbonara

TIP: Since this moves quickly, have all ingredients ready, close at hand. Have a hot dish for tossing and hot bowls to receive individual portions.

¼ pound pancetta—Italian style bacon—cut into 1" lengths
3 tablespoons olive oil
1 medium onion, finely chopped
1 pound fettuccine, freshly made
½ cup chopped parsley
1 cup finely diced Fontina cheese
1 cup freshly grated imported Italian Parmesan cheese
2 egg yolks, lightly beaten
Salt and freshly ground black pepper
Hot red pepper flakes

1. Cook bacon in skillet, stirring frequently, until crisp. Remove with slotted spoon and place on paper towel to drain.
2. Pour off most of fat from pan. Add olive oil and cook onion until tender and browned. Set aside until needed.
3. Cook fettuccine until just done. Drain thoroughly in large colander, lifting strands with 2 forks to make sure all water runs off. Turn into hot bowl.
4. Add onion, bacon, parsley, Fontina, ½ cup Parmesan, and yolks. Toss. The heat of the pasta will cook raw eggs on contact.
5. Add salt, freshly ground pepper and red pepper flakes to taste.
6. Serve pasta at once. Pass remaining Parmesan cheese and a pepper mill.

Branzino alla Zoni

3 pounds red snapper filets
1½ cups sliced mushrooms
4 tablespoons butter
⅓ cup dry white wine or vermouth
⅓ cup lemon juice
2 tablespoons chopped parsley
Pinch cinnamon
Garnish: 2 tablespoons toasted pine nuts
   2 oranges, peeled, cut into halves and sliced

1. Sauté snapper filets and mushrooms in butter until half done.
2. Add wine and lemon juice and cook a bit longer. Toss in remaining ingredients and cover for a minute or so.
3. When the fish is done, serve with mushrooms, pine nuts and orange pieces piled on top.

Filleta alla Cacciatore
(Tenderloin Steak, Hunter Style)

1 ounce dried boletus mushrooms
¾ cup very thin onion slices
5 tablespoons fruity olive oil
¾ cup dry red wine
¾ cup fresh tomatoes chopped with their juice
Salt and freshly ground pepper
6 8-ounce tenderloins, butterflied

1. Soak mushrooms at least 30 minutes with scant 2 cups lukewarm water. Lift out carefully without stirring up water. Rinse in several changes of cold water to remove any clinging grit. Cut into large pieces and reserve.
2. Filter soaking water through fine wire strainer lined with paper towel; reserve.
3. Brown onions in oil. Add mushrooms and soaking water. Cook until water is evaporated. Add wine and cook until it bubbles away; you must stir frequently. Add tomatoes and cook on low heat until oil separates from tomatoes. Add salt and freshly ground pepper to taste.
4. Sear steaks over high heat in olive oil, leaving rare. Remove to warm platter. Add sauce with a bit more wine if needed for deglazing. Pour over steaks and serve.

Carote al Burro e Formaggio

2 large bunches carrots, peeled and sliced ½" thick
5 tablespoons unsalted butter
Salt and freshly ground pepper
¼ teaspoon sugar
3 tablespoons imported Italian Parmesan cheese

1. Place carrots in a single layer in a heavy skillet; add butter. Add water almost level with carrots and cook over medium heat, uncovered.
2. When liquid has evaporated, add salt, pepper and sugar. Cook on low heat about an hour, until carrots are well-browned and quite reduced in volume. You may have to add a bit of water if carrots are not completely tender before they are browned. Carrot flavor will intensify.
3. Add grated Parmesan cheese, stir and serve.

Carrots may be prepared ahead and reheated, but don't add the cheese until carrots are about to be served.

Patate Arrosto

3 tablespoons unsalted butter
3 tablespoons fruity olive oil
1½ pounds new potatoes, cut into large chunks
Salt
Freshly ground pepper
Fresh rosemary and thyme

1. Preheat oven to 400 degrees.
2. Melt butter with olive oil, and pour over potatoes, tossing to make sure they are well covered.
3. Sprinkle with salt, pepper and chopped fresh rosemary and thyme.
4. Bake in preheated oven about 40 minutes, tossing once or twice along the way, until brown and crisp.

The proportions for **Patate Arrosto** *are unimportant. Fresh herbs are much better than dry for this recipe, and can be used in abundance since these potatoes are always served with aggressively flavored entrées.*

Boccone Dolce
(Sweet Mouthful)

6 egg whites
Salt
¼ teaspoon cream of tartar
1½ cups sugar
6 ounces semisweet chocolate
2½ cups whipping cream
2 pints strawberries

1. Preheat oven to 250 degrees.
2. Beat egg whites with pinch of salt until foamy. Add cream of tartar and beat until soft peaks form.
3. Very gradually beat in sugar to form a glossy meringue; texture and appearance should be similar to cosmetic cold cream.
4. Line baking sheets with parchment or waxed paper. Using an 8" cake pan, trace 3 circles. Use spatula to spread meringue evenly over circles.
5. Bake in preheated oven 1 hour. Let meringues dry in oven an hour longer. The meringues shouldn't turn color beyond a very pale gold; if they begin to darken, prop oven door open.
6. Remove meringues from oven and carefully peel off paper. Handling gently, set on racks to cool.
7. Melt chocolate with 3 tablespoons water in a double boiler. Spread over meringues. Make sure chocolate cools thoroughly on discs before continuing.
8. Slice berries, reserving 8 lovely ones with hulls for decoration.
9. Whip cream until stiff.
10. Place 1 chocolate-iced disc on serving plate and spread with thick layer of whipped cream. Cover with half of the sliced berries. Repeat with second chocolate meringue. Place white meringue on top and spread with whipped cream.
11. Pipe on a fancy border of whipped cream using a pastry bag. Arrange whole berries around edge so bright red and green form a brilliant contrast to the white cream and meringue. Keep in refrigerator until ready to serve.

TIP: If you like a crisp cookie-like meringue, you might keep it drying longer than an hour.

Henry Thiele

Dinner for Six

Top Hats

German Pot Roast

Potato Pancakes

Princess Charlotte Pudding

Wines:

With Top Hats—Duff Gordon Amontillado Sherry
With Roast—Christian Brothers Cabernet Sauvignon

Margaret Thiele, Owner
Wally Sperry, Chef

A history of Henry Thiele's in Portland is as much a tribute to a beloved man as to his excellent restaurant. Although Thiele has been gone since 1952, traditions are stoutly maintained by his widow Margaret and 34-year Thiele veteran, head chef Wally Sperry.

Margaret Thiele recalls her husband's colorful life from his beginnings in a little town in Germany, through training at hotels in Berlin, Paris and London, and on to New York at the Waldorf in 1904. He went on to Chicago, then to open the Fairmont Hotel in San Francisco—delayed a year by the Great Earthquake!—and settled finally in Portland.

Henry operated restaurants after the war, as well as a fleet of motorcycles which delivered 25-cent box lunches to the factories and the docks. He earned a reputation for the finest wedding catering and cakes in town: "In those days," muses Mrs. Thiele, "if Henry Thiele didn't do your wedding, you weren't married in Portland!"

The Depression ruined Henry's business, but not Henry. Building the present restaurant on a shoestring and opening as "a simple sandwich shop" on Henry's 50th birthday—right in the middle of the Depression—the Thieles were successful once again. Portland, remembering his talents, demanded more than sandwiches. Henry responded by not only giving Portland fine catering and an excellent restaurant, but by becoming a community leader and benefactor. Although stern and exacting as an employer (he lined up his staff every day for inspection), Henry Thiele was a gregarious man—a man who took time to come out to the dining room to talk to people, who carried tokens and gifts in his pockets for children—and a well-remembered practical joker.

Margaret Thiele has put all her efforts into keeping the 325-seat restaurant as much as possible as it was in Henry's time; many of her clientele can remember the "old days". A number of the staff have been with her for many years. Wally Sperry, who began in 1945, combines tremendous organization and long hours of hard work at a job he obviously loves to execute the huge, daily-changing menu of fresh, home-cooked food still featuring some of the specialties of Henry Thiele's German background.

2305 W. Burnside

Top Hats

12 slices dark bread
¾ cup butter
1½ cups grated Parmesan cheese
1 onion, very finely chopped
2 cups mayonnaise
Paprika
Garnish: tomato wedges
parsley sprigs

1. Cut bread into 2" rounds. Toast lightly.
2. Combine butter with ½ cup Parmesan. Spread on toasts. Dip in chopped onion.
3. Preheat broiler.
4. Combine mayonnaise with remaining Parmesan. Using a pastry bag with a star tip, pipe mixture around each toast round. Sprinkle with paprika.
5. Pass under broiler just until golden. Arrange attractively on a platter and garnish with tomato wedges and parsley sprigs.

German Pot Roast

1 4-pound beef roast
Brine
Brown Sauce
3 tablespoons apple or currant jelly
Potato Pancakes
Homemade applesauce

1. Marinate roast in **Brine** in refrigerator 7 days, turning once or twice a day.
2. Preheat oven to 400 degrees.
3. Roast beef 30 minutes or until beef is light brown on all sides. Remove from oven.
4. Reduce temperature to 300 degrees and pour off all juices in pan and discard.
5. Put roast in deep pan and pour in **Brown Sauce**. Sauce should cover ⅔ of roast. Roast until tender, about 2½ hours, depending on type and weight of meat. To test for tenderness, use 2-pronged fork. It should enter and retract easily.
6. Remove roast from pan and strain sauce. Add jelly and stir with whip until jelly melts and blends well. Sauce should have a slight sweet and sour flavor.
7. Serve at once with **Potato Pancakes** and homemade applesauce.

BRINE

2 quarts water
1 pint vinegar
1 teaspoon salt
½ teaspoon black pepper
½ cup mixed pickling spice
2 bay leaves
½ teaspoon monosodium glutamate—optional
1 medium onion, diced
1 carrot, diced
2 celery stalks, diced
¼ teaspoon each: garlic salt, onion salt, dry mustard, paprika, celery salt, allspice, cloves

Combine all ingredients.

BROWN SAUCE

1 medium onion, diced
1 clove garlic, diced
2 ounces oil
Flour
1 teaspoon paprika
1½ quarts beef stock
Salt and pepper

1. In a saucepan sauté onion and garlic in oil till light brown.
2. Add enough flour to make a thin roux; simmer 1 minute.
3. Add paprika and then beef stock, whisking. Simmer until smooth; add salt and pepper to taste.

Potato Pancakes

4 medium potatoes
1 medium onion
2 eggs
¼ cup milk
Salt and pepper to taste
Flour
Parsley or chives
Oil for frying

1. Medium-grind potatoes and onion in a food grinder, or shred in a food processor.
2. Add eggs, milk, salt and pepper. Stir in enough flour to thicken batter; then add parsley or chives.
3. Fry pancakes in oil until brown on both sides, using enough oil that pancakes move around with ease.
4. Garnish with parsley or chives

Princess Charlotte Pudding

1 pint milk
½ cup plus 2 tablespoons sugar
1 tablespoon cornstarch
2 eggs
½ envelope Knox unflavored gelatin
2 ounces water
½ cup whipping cream
Vanilla extract
6 to 8 medium almonds, roasted and chopped
Tart fruit juice, such as raspberry, strawberry, or loganberry

1. Mix milk, ½ cup sugar, cornstarch, and eggs in the top of a double boiler.
2. Cook, stirring well, until it becomes very smooth and thickened to custard cream consistency.
3. Allow to cool to 60 degrees.
4. Dissolve gelatin in water. Heat a little to dissolve thoroughly. Add to custard and cook, stirring, until it begins to set. Set aside until needed.
5. Beat whipping cream until firm and sweeten with remaining sugar to taste and a little vanilla.
6. Fold whipped cream and almonds gently into custard. Fill 6 individual molds or a 1-quart mold; let cool briefly, then refrigerate 4 to 5 hours.
7. Unmold custard and serve with the fruit juice poured over it.

Probably half of the people who come in here order **Princess Charlotte Pudding** *and I have never heard a complaint about it in all these years.*

Dinner for Six

Cream of Turkey Soup

Cole Slaw

Roast Turkey with Sage Dressing and Gravy

Bread Pudding

Spanish Coffee

Wines:

Chassagne Montrachet, '76
B.V. Cabernet Sauvignon, '75

Andrew and Amy Louie Owners
Jim Louie, Manager
Dave Louie, Head Chef

An old Portland tradition established in 1897 as a men's bar, Huber's has been in the same location inside the Oregon Pioneer Building since 1910.

Present owner Andrew Louie grew up with Huber's. At the turn of the century his Uncle Jim was chef, becoming manager in 1914 and half-owner in 1940. When Jim Louie died in 1946, Andrew and his family took over. He and his wife taught the restaurant's techniques to their sons Dave—who is now head chef—and Jim, who, besides managing the restaurant with a smooth and friendly spirit, is a genius at the art of making a Spanish coffee.

In such a long-established restaurant there are bound to be many changes. "When Huber's was a men's bar in the old days," Jim relates, "a man would come in, order a drink and get a free turkey or baked ham sandwich with it. Prohibition changed that: a man would come in and order a *sandwich*, and with that get a free *drink*. My father talks about Manhattans being served in coffee cups."

The menu remains the same at Huber's; they are known for their roast turkey and baked ham. And the comfortable atmosphere hasn't changed; when the sun is out, it pours through the stained glass windows, adding a glow to the dark-wooded interior.

320 SW Stark Street

Cream of Turkey Soup

1 carrot, diced
2 onions, diced
1 stalk celery, diced
6 tablespoons butter
2 tablespoons flour
3 cups turkey broth
1 bay leaf
1 cup milk, heated
½ cup diced turkey meat
Salt and pepper to taste

1. Sauté diced vegetables in butter in a large saucepan.
2. Add flour and cook 8 to 10 minutes, being careful not to brown.
3. Add broth gradually, stirring until slightly thickened and smooth.
4. Add bay leaf, simmer 30 minutes, then remove bay leaf.
5. Add heated milk and diced turkey meat. Season with salt and pepper. Serve.

Cole Slaw

1 cup vinegar
½ teaspoon Colman's mustard
¼ teaspoon white pepper
¾ teaspoon salt
2 cups sugar
2 cups mayonnaise
2 pounds cabbage, finely chopped

1. With mixer at slow speed combine vinegar, mustard, white pepper, salt and sugar.
2. Add mayonnaise and beat until smooth.
3. Pour over cabbage and marinate at least 1 hour.
4. Serve on chilled individual salad plates.

Roast Turkey with Sage Dressing and Gravy

Make **Sage Dressing** *first and hold in refrigerator until needed.*

1 10-pound turkey
Salt
½ cup butter, melted
Poultry seasoning
4 cups water
Sage Dressing
Gravy

1. Preheat oven to 350 degrees.
2. Clean turkey inside and out. Pat with paper towels. Rub inside and out with salt.
3. Fill cavity with **Sage Dressing.**
4. Place turkey on a roasting rack and set in a flat pan with 3" sides.
5. Brush all over with melted butter and sprinkle with poultry seasoning.
6. Pour water into roasting pan. Cover turkey legs and breast with foil. Cook in preheated oven 3 hours, basting every half hour. To test for doneness, insert a knife into the second joint between leg and breast; turkey is done when the juices are clear. Also: check the internal temperature of the bird by sticking a thermometer into the thickest part of the breast. It should read 180 degrees when turkey is done.

SAGE DRESSING

1 cup chopped onion
2 cups chopped celery
6 tablespoons butter
12 cups croutons—or dried bread, crushed
2 tablespoons salt
½ teaspoon pepper
¼ teaspoon rosemary
¼ teaspoon tarragon leaves
¼ teaspoon marjoram
1 cup turkey broth
Raisins—optional

1. Sauté onions and celery in butter and pour over bread cubes.
2. Add seasonings to broth and pour over bread and vegetable mixture. Mix ingredients together well, adding raisins if desired. Refrigerate if turkey is not ready to receive stuffing.
3. Push dressing into turkey cavity, but do not pack or dressing will not be fluffy. If there is leftover dressing, or if you prefer not to stuff the turkey, you may steam the dressing separately for 20 minutes.

TIP: Broth can be prepared with the turkey giblets, onion and celery dice and desired seasoning simmered in water to cover, or canned broth may be substituted.

TURKEY GRAVY

¼ pound butter or turkey fat
2 to 3 tablespoons flour
2 to 3 cups turkey broth from the roasting pan
½ teaspoon soy sauce
Salt, pepper and granulated garlic to taste

1. Melt butter in a saucepan. Add flour, combining well with a whisk.
2. Add broth, stirring constantly until it thickens.
3. Add soy sauce, salt, pepper and granulated garlic.
4. Set over hot water until ready to serve.

Bread Pudding

3 eggs
3 cups milk
¾ cup sugar
2 slices dry bread, cut into 1" squares
½ teaspoon cinnamon
1 tablespoon melted butter

1. Preheat oven to 350 degrees.
2. Mix together eggs, milk and sugar, and pour into a casserole.
3. Add bread squares, pushing down into egg mixture.
4. Sprinkle cinnamon and melted butter over top of mixture.
5. Place casserole in a water bath; bake in preheated oven 45 minutes.

Spanish Coffee

Per serving—
Slice of lime
Sugar
¾ ounce Bacardi 151 Rum
2 ounces Kahlua
¾ ounce Triple Sec
Coffee
Heavy cream, lightly whipped
Pinch nutmeg

1. Moisten rim of glass with lime, then dip rim in sugar.
2. Pour in rum and ignite. Add Kahlua, Triple Sec and coffee.
3. Top with lightly whipped cream and a sprinkle of nutmeg.

INDIGINE

Antipasto with Salami

*Roast Chicken
with
Bleu Cheese and Shrimp Stuffing*

*Seasonal Fruit with Fresh Cream Cheese
or
Ginger Cheesecake*

*Millie Howe and Howard Waskow, Owners
Millie Howe, Chef*

Seating "fifteen skinny people, or ten fat people," the first Indigine was a real phenomenon in its six years as a sit-down restaurant: just four small tables accommodated the five-course Friday and Saturday night dinners and Sunday brunches—reservations for which had to be made a year in advance. Creative international dishes colorfully presented with love and dedication by co-owners Howard Waskow and Millie Howe won a reputation which follows them into their new format, introduced in December 1978. Their very name, Indigine, synthesizes "indigenous," representing their commitment to fresh, local products—a sort of seasonal, regional approach—and "Antigone," the Greek heroine who was as forthright and courageous as they hope to be with their food.

Indigine has been re-opened as a continental-inspired gourmet shop long familiar to the East Coast, but new to the Pacific Northwest. Portlanders now enjoy the busy Euorpean housewife's tradition of relying upon *charcuteries* and *salumerie* and pastry shops for pâtés, fine sausages and sumptuous pastries to supplement home-cooked meals. Friday and Saturday afternoons—the only hours of operation—find former diners dropping by for a simple cinnamon roll, a half-pound bagel... or perhaps to make a meal of varied pâtés and terrines: lamb with chutney, Cuban black bean, dilled shrimp. Cold salads served with sourdough bread, James Beard-inspired brownies, wonderful cakes and tarts are ready to take out. Paella salad, *frutti di mare*—Italian seafood salad with squid—and homemade cream cheese are among Millie's presentations, bringing her the appreciation of the increasingly sophisticated Portlander's palate.

3725 SE Division

Salami

5½ pounds lean ground beef
1 tablespoon freshly ground black pepper
1 tablespoon finely chopped garlic
2 teaspoons ground cumin
2 tablespoons brown sugar
2 tablespoons chili powder
4 tablespoons curing salt, e.g. Morton's Tender Quick
Ground small red chiles, to taste
¾ cup dry red wine

1. Mix all but wine very thoroughly with hands, not mixer.
2. Add wine. Refrigerate overnight.
3. Preheat oven to 250 degrees.
4. Divide meat mixture into quarters and roll into salami shapes about 10" long. Wrap in cheesecloth and tie securely.
5. Bake on rack in roasting pan 4 hours. Turn frequently to prevent flattening.
6. Cool 15 minutes, then remove cheesecloth. Cool completely. Wrap in good quality plastic wrap.

TIP: Recipe makes four 1-pound salamis.

Fresh Cream Cheese

1 quart whipping cream
1 quart half-and-half
2 cups buttermilk
1 tablespoon salt

1. Combine all ingredients. Place over medium heat, stirring occasionally.
2. When curds form at 215 degrees, gently transfer to a colander lined with 4 layers of moistened cheesecloth.
3. Drain until center is firm, then twist ends of cheesecloth together and transfer to sieve or other cheese mold. Cover tightly and refrigerate overnight.
4. The next day peel back twisted cheesecloth. Invert cheese onto plate. Remove sieve and remaining layers of cheesecloth.
5. Serve with bagels, or as a dessert cheese with fresh fruit.

Roast Chicken with Bleu Cheese and Shrimp Stuffing

1 3½- to 4-pound frying chicken
8 ounces bleu cheese
1½ sticks softened, unsalted butter
4 ounces fresh cream cheese
8 ounces baby shrimp meat
3 tablespoons lemon juice
Parsley, chopped, to taste
Chives, chopped, to taste
Salt and freshly ground black pepper
16 cloves garlic, coarsely chopped

1. Preheat oven to 450 degrees.
2. Butterfly chicken by cutting through backbone from tail to neck. Invert and flatten by cracking breast bones.
3. Gently loosen skin, starting at breast end, by inserting hand like a glove. Loosen all the way through to legs, trying to leave skin at cut edges intact.
4. Mix bleu cheese, one stick butter, cream cheese, shrimp, lemon juice, parsley and chives. Distribute mixture into area under skin.
5. Sprinkle salt and pepper on underside of chicken. Place on a bed of chopped garlic and slather with remaining butter, melted.
6. Roast about 1 hour or until nicely puffed and browned. To serve, cut into quarters with kitchen shears.

Fresh Ginger Cheesecake

1 16-ounce package graham crackers, crushed
1 teaspoon cinnamon
1¼ cups sugar
¼ cup melted butter, plus butter for pan
24 ounces cream cheese
1 cup sour cream
6 egg yolks
1 teaspoon vanilla extract
1 tablespoon lemon juice
½ cup peeled and finely chopped fresh ginger
1 cup plus 2 tablespoons flour
6 egg whites
½ teaspoon cream of tartar

1. Preheat oven to 350 degrees.
2. Combine graham cracker crumbs, cinnamon, ¼ cup sugar and and butter.
3. Butter a 10" springform pan. Press crust mixture into bottom and sides of pan. Chill.
4. Mix cream cheese and sour cream. Add yolks, vanilla, lemon juice, ginger, remaining sugar and flour.
5. Whisk egg whites with cream of tartar until stiff. Fold into cream cheese mixture and pour into chilled springform.
6. Bake 1 hour 10 minutes. Cool, then chill before serving.

Dinner for Four

Crawfish Appetizers

Crab Legs Kasseri with Rice

Salad with Jake's Dressing

Cheesecake

Wines:

With Crawfish—Eyrie Vineyards Sauvignon Blanc
With Crab Legs—Hillcrest or Ponzi White Riesling

William McCormic, Owner
Jim Barklow, Executive Chef

A part of Portland history, Jake's has occupied its present location since 1908. The decor is a combination of the old and new: dark wood and shiny brass; historical paintings and photographs; quips and interesting articles decking the walls; waiters wearing white jackets and black trousers and ties. There are several dining areas and two bars; the front bar normally bustles while the 1220 Room at the back of the restaurant offers a quieter atmosphere.

Head chef James Barklow graduated several years ago from the Culinary Institute of America in New York, working in several restaurants since. His menu at Jake's offers mainly seafood. By way of implementing the suggested menu for *Dining In—Portland*, Jim tells us that crawfish are in season from April first through late September. "Since they're found in most rivers and streams, if the trout fishing is slow, try your luck in catching crawfish for dinner instead."

Within the past year, Jake's has extended its wine list to include a large selection of Oregon wines, with the house wine now an Oregonian.

SW 12th & Stark Streets

Crawfish Appetizers

2 quarts water
4 tablespoons salt
4 tablespoons pickling spice
4 tablespoons cayenne pepper
1 ounce Tabasco
2 tablespoons dry mustard
1 pint malt vinegar
2 tablespoons granulated garlic
20 crawfish

1. Combine all ingredients except crawfish; boil 15 minutes.
2. Add live crawfish. When stock returns to a boil, cook crawfish just 1 minute longer.
3. Remove crawfish immediately to cold water to stop cooking process.
4. Arrange on a platter and serve.

Often crawfish have a natural bacteria growing on them; it is not harmful but, in order to insure that the crawfish will not spoil when stored for more than a day, it is a good idea to store them in a chilled brine. One such is a simple solution of four tablespoons salt to two quarts water.

Crab Legs Kasseri

1 quart milk
½ teaspoon white pepper
1½ teaspoons dry mustard
5 dashes Tabasco
1 teaspoon salt
4 tablespoons butter
4 tablespoons flour
½ pound cold pack Cheddar cheese
½ cup grated Parmesan cheese
⅓ cup sherry
⅓ cup beer
1 cup sliced mushrooms
24 crab legs
¾ cup chopped green onions
½ cup grated Kasseri cheese
Grated Parmesan cheese for topping
Rice

1. Preheat oven to 425 degrees.
2. Combine milk, pepper, mustard, Tabasco and salt in the top of a double boiler, and heat.
3. Make a roux by melting butter, adding flour and cooking over a low heat until bubbly. Add to hot milk mixture.
4. When mixture thickens, add Cheddar and Parmesan. Allow cheeses to melt; add sherry and beer. Remove from heat.
5. Line bottoms of 4 individual casserole dishes with scatterings of mushrooms and green onions.
6. Place 6 crab legs in each dish; top with Kasseri.
7. Divide cheese sauce over crab legs; top with grated Parmesan.
8. Bake in preheated oven 15 to 20 minutes, or until golden brown.
9. Spoon over **Rice**.

The cheese-mustard sauce in this recipe may be stored up to a week under refrigeration.

RICE

¼ pound bacon, minced
¼ cup minced onion
¼ cup minced celery
2 cups regular rice
3 cups hot chicken stock
1 teaspoon thyme
2 teaspoons marjoram
1 teaspoon granulated garlic
¼ cup minced mushrooms
Salt to taste

1. Preheat oven to 375 degrees.
2. Sauté bacon until crisp. Add onions and celery and sauté 1 minute more.
3. Add rice, stirring to make sure all gets coated with bacon fat.
4. Season hot chicken broth with thyme, marjoram and garlic; pour over rice. Add mushrooms.
5. Bring to a boil, cover, and place in preheated oven 18 minutes. Remove from oven and let stand, covered, 30 minutes before serving.

Salad with Jake's Dressing

Fresh salad greens, washed and torn
Jake's Dressing
Croutons

Prepare salad greens. Toss with **Jake's Dressing** and top with croutons.

JAKE'S DRESSING

2 eggs
1 teaspoon salt
2 tablespoons granulated garlic
1 teaspoon white pepper
2 tablespoons sugar
1 tablespoon dry mustard
2 teaspoons basil
1 teaspoon oregano
1 teaspoon Worcestershire
1 quart oil
⅓ cup cider vinegar
2½ teaspoons lemon juice

1. Combine eggs and all dry ingredients in a blender at medium speed. Add Worcestershire.
2. Slowly add oil. When dressing becomes thick, balance with a little vinegar to thin.
3. Continue to alternate oil and vinegar until entirely incorporated. Add lemon juice.

Cheesecake

1½ pounds cream cheese
1¼ cups sugar
4 eggs
1 teaspoon vanilla extract
1 tablespoon grated lemon rind
Pinch salt
1 ounce orange juice
1 ounce Grand Marnier
4 tablespoons flour
Butter to prepare pan
Topping

1. Preheat oven to 325 degrees.
2. Blend cream cheese and sugar until smooth with mixer at low speed. Add eggs, 1 at a time, mixing well after each addition.
3. Add lemon rind, vanilla and salt. Continue mixing 15 minutes.
4. Add orange juice and Grand Marnier. Stir in 3 tablespoons flour.
5. Butter a 9" springform pan; sprinkle in remaining flour, then shake out excess. Pour in batter and bake in preheated oven 1 hour, or until center has set.
6. Cover cake with **Topping** and return to oven 5 minutes.
7. Cool 1 hour. Place in refrigerator until well chilled.

TOPPING

½ pint sour cream
2 tablespoons sugar
½ teaspoon vanilla extract

Combine ingredients thoroughly.

This cheesecake is especially nice served with fresh fruit of the season.

L'Auberge

Dinner for Six

Pâté

Potage Velouté aux Chanterelles

Moules et Crevettes à la Marinière

Poulet au Beurre

Pot de Crème au Chocolat

Wines:

With Pâté, Potage and Moules—Meursault-Perrieres, '73
With Poulet—Chambolle-Musigny "Amoureuses," '71
With Pot de Crème—Château Filhot, '71

Bill McLaughlin, Owner
June Reznikoff, Head Chef

The simple decor and size of L'Auberge—tables and chairs lining the walls of the narrow room with seating for thirty—enhance rather than inhibit the talents of owner Bill McLaughlin and head chef June Reznikoff.

McLaughlin acquired L'Auberge in 1976, veering from his career as teacher of philosophy at Reed College and Portland State University, with a side line of serious painting. Bringing the same dedication to his restaurant, McLaughlin soon evolved the philosophy that all concerned must know what is expected in each position. He claims that "each employee at L'Auberge starts out as a dishwasher," and McLaughlin himself still busses and waits tables two nights a week.

L'Auberge has recently initiated a Sunday brunch in addition to their exquisite dinners.

2180 W. Burnside

Pâté

Prepare **Panade** *and* **Spice Mixture** *before beginning Pâté.*

¾ pound pork fat, cut into chunks
½ pound chicken and/or duck livers
¼ pound lean pork and/or veal and/or chicken
1 to 2 eggs
1 tablespoon brandy
1 teaspoon salt
Panade
1 teaspoon **Ground Spice Mixture**
Sprig thyme
Bay leaf
Garnish: cornichons

1. Preheat oven to 350 degrees.
2. Grind all ingredients together.
3. Pour mixture into terrine.
4. Top with thyme and bay leaf.
5. Cover and bake in a water bath in preheated oven about 1¼ hours, or until 160 degrees when tested with a thermometer. Remove from oven, top with a weight, and allow to cool.
6. Refrigerate until ready to serve.
7. Cut pâté into slices and garnish with cornichons.

The pâté should be prepared several days ahead of time for the best flavor. Serve with freshly made French bread.

PANADE

⅓ cup white rice
1 cup beef stock
3 tablespoons duck fat or butter

1. Simmer all ingredients together until tender.
2. Set aside and let cool until needed.

SPICE MIXTURE

Thoroughly mix together even amounts of clove, mace, nutmeg, paprika, thyme, basil, cinnamon, marjoram, sage, savory and pepper.

Potage Velouté aux Chanterelles

2 cups chanterelles, very finely chopped
1½ cups heavy cream
1¼ cups chicken broth
1¼ cups fish stock
Salt and pepper to taste

1. Place chanterelles in a saucepan and cover with heavy cream. Simmer very slowly 1 hour, stirring occasionally.
2. Add chicken and fish stocks. Simmer to allow flavors to blend.
3. Add salt and pepper to taste.

TIP: This soup may be made with commercial mushrooms and may be thickened with a roux if desired.

Moules et Crevettes à la Marinière

2 quarts mussels
2 pounds shrimp
1½ cups white wine
2 shallots, chopped
Several sprigs parsley
Bay leaf
Pinch thyme
1½ tablespoons butter
1½ tablespoons flour
Garnish: chopped parsley

1. Wash and scrub mussels thoroughly.
2. Peel and devein shrimp, leaving the last shell segments attached.
3. In a large saucepan put wine, shallots, parsley sprigs, bay leaf and thyme.
4. Add cleaned mussels to the saucepan; steam until all mussels have opened. Remove with slotted spoon.
5. Strain remaining liquid into another saucepan and bring to a boil.
6. Drop shrimp into boiling liquid for a few minutes. Lift from liquid and set aside.
7. Cream flour and butter together; add to remaining hot liquid. Stir until smooth, and reduce slightly.
8. Place mussels in their half shells. Arrange on a serving plate with shrimp.
9. Pour reduced liquid over mussels and shrimp. Sprinkle with chopped parsley and serve hot.

Poulet au Beurre

1 whole bodied frying chicken
¼ pound butter
2 garlic cloves, peeled and minced
4 shallots, finely chopped
1 tablespoon chopped chives
1 tablespoon chopped parsley
1 teaspoon thyme
¼ cup chopped mushrooms—optional
2 tablespoons brandy
½ to 1 cup breadcrumbs—and/or optional ground toasted filberts
Salt
Pepper
Chicken stock for deglazing

1. Preheat oven to 400 degrees.
2. Loosen skin on chicken breasts, thighs and legs.
3. Mix together in a bowl the butter, garlic, shallots, chives, parsley, thyme, chopped mushrooms if desired, brandy, breadcrumbs, filberts if desired, and salt and pepper to taste.
4. Push mixture under skin of chicken, being careful not to tear skin.
5. Salt and pepper cavity of chicken and loosely fill with any extra stuffing. Truss.
6. Bake in preheated oven about 1 hour.
7. When juices run clear and chicken is brown, remove from oven.
8. Cut into serving pieces.
9. Quickly deglaze pan with some chicken stock; skim off extra fat from roasting juices. Pour juice over chicken and serve.

Pot de Crème au Chocolat

2 cups heavy cream
4 ounces bittersweet chocolate
¼ cup sugar
½ vanilla bean, scraped
6 egg yolks
2 tablespoons brandy or rum
Garnish: sweetened whipped cream

1. Preheat oven to 300 degrees.
2. Bring cream, chocolate, sugar, and scraped vanilla bean to a simmer, stirring until completely smooth.
3. In a bowl, beat egg yolks thoroughly, but do not encourage a foam to form.
4. Carefully pour hot cream mixture over egg yolks, beating constantly.
5. Stir in brandy or rum.
6. Pour mixture through a fine strainer, then into individual custard cups, skimming off any foam.
7. Cover cups with individual lids or foil. Set in a water bath and bake in preheated oven ½ to 1 hour, or until each is firm. Remove from water bath and refrigerate until ready to serve.
8. Serve cold in the cups, garnished with rosettes of whipped cream.

Dinner for Eight

Pâté de Canard aux Pistaches

Bisque d'Ecrevisses

Saumon en Croûte Val de Loire
Sauce Bercy

Julienne de Legume Almandine

Parfait aux Framboises

Wines:

With Pâté—Domaine G. Brun Morgon
With Bisque—L. Latour Meursault, '73
With Salmon—Chassagne-Montrachet, '73
With Parfait—Château Lafon Contigu a Yquem, '75

Linda Menager, Owner
Pierre Auroy, Head Chef

When Linda Menager reopened L'Escargot, an intimate restaurant seating just thirty-five diners, her long-time good friend, Pierre Auroy, came up from San Francisco to become the head chef.

Pierre began cooking at age fourteen in Bourges, a city in central France, at the restaurant Jacques Coeur. Three years later, he went to Paris to work at the restaurant in the Eiffle Tower. From Paris, Pierre went to Montreal and from there to Washington, D.C., where he worked the kitchens of San Soucis and Rive Gauche. His time in San Francisco, just before coming to L'Escargot in Portland, was spent cooking for Le Camembert and Victor's in the St. Francis Hotel.

L'Escargot's lunchtime tables are covered with calicos and fresh flowers. At dinner the decor changes to linen and candles.

NW Kearney and NW 20th

Pâté de Canard aux Pistaches
(Duck Pâté with Pistachios)

1 duck, 2¼ pounds, with liver and giblet
3 ounces port wine
1 pound veal shoulder
1 pound pork shoulder
1 ounce white wine
1 ounce brandy
Pinch thyme
Bay leaf
Dash Four Seasoning Spice
Salt and pepper
3 eggs
2 ounces pistachios
Thin slices pork fat to line mold

1. Bone the duck. Remove breast and cut into strips. Marinate in 1 ounce of port.
2. Cut remainder of duck and the veal and pork into chunks; marinate with 1 ounce of port, white wine, brandy, thyme, bay leaf and Four Seasoning Spice for at least 6 hours.
3. After marinating, grind the meat. Add marinade, eggs, pistachios, salt and pepper. Mix well.
4. Preheat oven to 400 degrees.
5. Line a mold or terrine with thin slices of pork fat. Fill half full with ground meat mixture. Put a layer of duck breast pieces on top and cover with remaining ground meat mixture.
6. Cook pâté in a water bath in preheated oven 40 minutes.
7. When finished, leave in mold with a flat weight on top until cool. Cut in slices and serve.

By putting the weight on top after the pâté has cooked, you eliminate the chance of hiding any air pockets.

Bisque d'Ecrevisses
(Crayfish Soup)

1 onion, diced
2 carrots, diced
1 stalk celery, diced
1 clove garlic
6 ounces butter
1 teaspoon tarragon
Bouquet garni (parsley, bay leaf and thyme tied together)
30 crayfish, well washed
2 ounces brandy
2 glasses white wine
5 cups fish stock
Salt, pepper and paprika
½ cup rice
1 cup whipping cream

1. Lightly sauté onions, carrots, celery and garlic in butter. Add tarragon and bouquet garni.
2. Add well washed crayfish and stir until shells turn bright red.
3. Add brandy and flame. Pour in white wine and fish stock and cook 10 minutes. Add a pinch each of salt, pepper and paprika, and cook 10 minutes.
4. Cook rice separately in water 18 minutes. Strain.
5. Remove tails from crayfish and reserve for garnish.
6. Add cooked rice to crayfish and stock mixture. Cook 15 minutes.
7. Grind mixture and strain through a fine strainer. Add cream and bring to a boil.
8. Serve garnished with peeled crayfish tails.

Saumon en Croûte Val de Loire, Sauce Beurre Bercy

2-pound salmon filet
1 sheet puff pastry dough
2 bunches spinach
½ cup mushrooms, sliced
1 glass white wine
¼ cup rice, cooked
3 eggs, hard-cooked
Salt, pepper and thyme
Sauce Beurre Bercy

1. Blanch spinach in salted water. Drain, squeeze dry, and chop.
2. Lightly simmer sliced mushrooms in wine. Strain, reserving wine for sauce.
3. Combine chopped spinach, mushrooms and cooked rice; season with salt, pepper and thyme.
4. Cut filet lengthwise evenly. Place 1 piece of salmon in the center of rolled rectangle of puff pastry. Cover with spinach mixture and sliced hard-cooked eggs. Top with remaining piece of salmon.
5. Preheat oven to 375 degrees.
6. Wet edges of dough lightly; pull them over salmon, giving a loaf-like shape. Pinch dampened edges together to make pastry seams stick together.
7. Roll "loaf" over, seam side down, onto a baking sheet. Make a small hole on top with a knife and brush surface with beaten egg. (The hole in the pastry allows the steam to escape during cooking.)
8. Bake in preheated oven 20 minutes. Slice and serve with **Sauce Beurre Bercy.**

SAUCE BEURRE BERCY

½ ounce chopped shallots
6 ounces butter
Wine reserved from cooked mushrooms
Salt and pepper to taste

1. Sauté shallots in 1 ounce butter until blond in color.
2. Add wine, salt and pepper. Reduce volume by ½; remove from heat.
3. Add butter in pieces, whisking until sauce is smooth. Serve separately.

Julienne de Legumes Almandine

2 carrots
2 turnips
1 stalk celery
2 zucchini
¼ cup sliced almonds
2 ounces butter
Salt and pepper

1. Cut carrots, turnips, celery and zucchini in julienne strips 2" long by ⅛" thick.
2. Blanch carrots and turnips separately; cool in cold water. Drain well.
3. Put butter in a frying pan. Sauté first the zucchini, then add carrots, turnips and celery. Add almonds last.
4. Sauté vegetables and almonds 2 minutes; season and serve.

Parfait aux Framboises
(Raspberry Parfait)

2 pounds fresh raspberries
10 ounces sugar
1 ounce kirsch
12 egg yolks
2 cups heavy cream, stiffly whipped

1. Cook raspberries gently with sugar a few minutes. Remove from heat and let cool. Strain, reserving berries for garnish.
2. Add juice to egg yolks in a mixing bowl placed in a water bath. Whip continuously until mixture becomes fluffy and stiff. Add kirsch.
3. Remove from water bath and continue whipping until mixture cools.
4. Fold in whipped cream. Add reserved berries and mix gently. Pour into sherbet glasses and place in freezer for 30 minutes before serving.

THE LONDON GRILL

Dinner for Six

Hot Artichoke with Hollandaise Sauce

Chilled Spring and Summer Cucumber Soup

*London Grill Dinner Salad
with House Dressing*

*Lamb Roast with Dijon Mustard, Herbs
and Grand Marnier*

Benson Coupe

Wines:

*With Artichoke, Soup, and Salad—
Cuvaison Chardonnay, '76
With Lamb—Ridge Selection Zinfandel, '77
With Coupe—Schramsberg Blanc de Blancs*

*The Benson
Xavier Bauser, Executive Chef*

The London Grill, named for a famous London restaurant of Dickens' era, and an integral part of the elegant sixty-six-year-old Benson Hotel, has purveyed award-winning cuisine and service in an atmosphere unchanged since 1955. Recently deemed in need of both remodeling and a lightening-up of atmosphere and menu, the new London Grill re-opened in December of 1978 as a triumph of traditional design and comfort. Vaulted ceilings and original oak paneling have been retained, now complemented by rich red and brown leathers, huge chandeliers and mirrors, upholstered chairs and loveseats, hunting scenes, silver, brass and copper in abundance, and gold-colored table linens. An eighteenth-century English polished steel fireplace is perhaps the greatest "new" treasure. Excellent service by a large and highly-trained staff completes the roster of treasures.

Swiss-born executive chef Xavier Bauser followed apprenticeship in Switzerland with a period with the Chalet Swiss restaurant organization in Holland. Since joining Western International Hotels in 1966, Bauser has been executive sous chef at The Georgia in Vancouver, B.C., then at the Benson and the Continental Plaza in Chicago, and was made executive chef at the Portland Benson in 1975.

Hotel guests as well as local patrons may well endorse director of restaurants Kaspar Murer's declared goal to be the best restaurant in Portland; the attempt to walk that proverbial tightrope between tradition's comforts and innovation's excitements has incorporated the best of both at the London Grill.

SW Broadway and SW Oak

Hot Artichoke with Hollandaise Sauce

1½ gallons water
Juice of 2 lemons
2 teaspoons salt
6 small to medium artichokes
Hollandaise Sauce
6 lemon slices

1. Place water, lemon juice and salt in pot and bring to a boil.
2. Meanwhile, cut off the stem at the base and approximately ½" of the tops of the artichokes. Wash thoroughly in cold water. Boil gently approximately 20 to 30 minutes in the lemon salt water. Check for doneness by poking bottoms with a fork. Remove artichokes and place upside down on a towel to drain a few minutes.
3. With a fork, lift out center leaves. Scratch out the center stringy core with a teaspoon, being careful not to scratch out the edible artichoke bottom.
4. Fill each artichoke with **Hollandaise Sauce** and serve on a hot plate. At the side of each table setting, place a plate for the leaves, a finger bowl with warm water, a slice of lemon and a napkin.

HOLLANDAISE SAUCE

1 pound butter
2 tablespoons white vinegar
2 tablespoons medium dry white table wine
¼ teaspoon broken black peppercorns
1 shallot, chopped
2 tablespoons water
4 egg yolks
Salt and pepper
Juice of ½ lemon
Worcestershire

1. To clarify butter, place in a casserole and melt over low heat. Simmer 15 to 30 minutes until clear and all solid parts have collected at the bottom. Keep removing foam from the top with a spoon or small ladle while simmering. Remove from heat and let rest, with casserole slightly tilted sideways, so sediment can collect at lower corner. Butter is now clarified.
2. Pour vinegar and wine into another casserole. Add broken peppercorns and shallot. Bring to a boil and simmer until hardly any liquid remains.
3. Remove from heat and add water. Strain into a stainless steel or heavy china bowl. Set bowl into hot—not boiling—water bath. Add yolks and beat with whisk until mass is firm and smooth. Be careful not to scramble eggs with too much heat.
4. Slowly add clarified butter with a ladle while stirring vigorously. Egg mass and butter should both be approximately the same temperature—120 degrees. If sauce gets too hot, add a few drops of cold water. Sauce should be thick, yet smooth-flowing.
5. Season to taste with salt, pepper, lemon juice and Worcestershire.

Spring and Summer Cucumber Soup

4 cups chicken stock
1 onion, chopped
4 cucumbers, peeled, seeds removed, sliced
1 large potato, peeled and sliced
Pinch fresh or dry dill
Salt and pepper
½ cup sweet or sour cream
Garnish: 6 sprigs fresh dill

1. Place chicken stock, onion, cucumber, potato, and pinch of dill in heatproof casserole. Bring to a boil and simmer until tender, 15 to 20 minutes.
2. Let cool to room temperature.
3. Pour into blender and blend to a creamy consistency. Season to taste with salt and pepper. Chill in refrigerator.
4. Before serving, add cream. Garnish with dill sprigs.

TIP: If too thick, thin with a little cold chicken stock.

London Grill Dinner Salad

2 medium-to-large heads butter lettuce
Garnish: 12 tomato slices
12 white asparagus spears
1⅛ cups **Vinaigrette Dressing**

1. Carefully separate lettuce leaves, removing stems and bad parts. Wash thoroughly in cold water. Place in a cloth; holding cloth by all four corners, swing lettuce dry. Chill in refrigerator.
2. Place lettuce leaves on chilled plates. Garnish each with 2 tomato slices and 2 asparagus spears. Distribute dressing evenly and serve immediately.

VINAIGRETTE DRESSING

½ onion, chopped
5 green onions, chopped
1 teaspoon chopped parsley
½ teaspoon Dijon mustard
1 hard-cooked egg, chopped
1 egg yolk
¼ cup cider vinegar
¾ cup vegetable oil
Salt and pepper
Worcestershire

1. Mix first 5 ingredients with egg yolk thoroughly.
2. Add vinegar and oil. Mix.
3. Season to taste with salt, pepper and Worcestershire. Mix well and store in refrigerator.

Lamb Roast with Dijon Mustard, Herbs and Grand Marnier

6 trimmed racks of lamb, 4 ribs approximately 12 ounces each
Marinade
Dijon mustard
Salt and pepper to taste
Vegetable oil
Sauce Robert
Fresh vegetables of your choice
Oven-browned potatoes
1 cup or more Grand Marnier

1. Marinate lamb 1 day in **Marinade**.
2. Remove and wipe dry. Spread with Dijon mustard and salt and pepper.
3. Preheat oven to 375 degrees.
4. Brown lamb quickly on both sides in oil in saucepan.
5. Roast in preheated oven 10 to 12 minutes. Remove from oven.
6. Carve rack into 2 equal chops. Serve with vegetables of choice and potatoes. Pass mustard sauce at the table. Serve a 1-ounce glass of Grand Marnier on the side—to be poured over lamb or drunk, according to diner's choice.

MARINADE

3/8 cup vegetable oil
3 tablespoons dry sherry
3 tablespoons medium dry white wine
1 onion, chopped
2 cloves garlic, chopped
1 teaspoon curry powder
1 teaspoon coriander
1 teaspoon salt
½ teaspoon ground pepper

Combine all ingredients and blend thoroughly.

SAUCE ROBERT (Mustard Sauce)

1 carrot
1 piece celery root same size as carrot, or substitute 1 celery stalk
1 medium onion
1 bay leaf
½ teaspoon cracked peppercorns
½ teaspoon rosemary
½ teaspoon thyme
4 tablespoons red table wine
1 teaspoon Dijon mustard
Freshly ground black pepper
1⅛ cups **Brown Veal Stock**

1. Cut vegetables into fingertip-sized cubes. Mix with bay leaf, cracked peppercorns, thyme and rosemary. Roast with lamb last 5 minutes.
2. When removing racks, deglaze pan with wine and reduce over medium heat.
3. Add Dijon mustard, ground pepper and **Brown Veal Stock**. Reduce over low heat to desired consistency. Salt to taste and serve with lamb.

BROWN VEAL STOCK

1 to 2 pounds meaty veal bones; chop (or have your butcher chop) into 2" to 3" pieces
1 carrot, scrubbed and quartered
1 onion, halved
Salt and pepper to taste
Parsley, thyme, bay leaf, garlic, leek as desired

1. Heat oven to 450 degrees.
2. Arrange bones and vegetables in roasting pan and brown in oven, turning occasionally, 30 minutes.
3. Drain fat. Transfer bones and vegetables to a kettle. Deglaze roasting pan with 1 cup water and add to kettle.
4. Add desired seasonings in small quantity. Cover with cold water. Bring to simmer. Skim any scum that rises to the surface. Simmer 4 to 5 hours.
5. Chill. Scrape off congealed fat. Taste stock. Reduce further if weak. This yields approximately a quart of stock.

Benson Coupe

1 apple
1 orange
1 banana
1 peach
Other seasonal fruit
1 fluid ounce Curaçao
2 fluid ounces whole cream, whipped
6 scoops strawberry ice cream
6 pineapple rings
3 strawberries, halved

1. Remove cores and pits of fruit, peel banana and cut all into ¼" pieces.
2. Marinate in Curaçao approximately 2 hours. Just before serving, mix in whipped cream, reserving small amount for garnish.
3. For each serving, place 1 scoop strawberry ice cream in chilled dessert glass, surround with marinated fruit salad, and top with a pineapple ring and ½ strawberry. Garnish with reserved whipped cream.

Dinner for Six

Mint Julep

Iced Mint Tea

Fresh Spinach Salad with Cafe House Dressing

Charleston Corn Soup

Oyster Pan Roast

Southern Candied Tomatoes

*Carolyn's Blueberry Pudding
with Lemon Wine Sauce*

*Tim and Tes Collett, Owners
Tim Collett, Head Chef
Gregg Lindsey, Chef*

When Tim and Tes Collett walked into the Post Office Pharmacy and Fountain in early 1978 to have a soda, they found comfortable surroundings, a varied clientele—and a desire to own the place. Two months later, they did. With some reconstruction and remodeling, and definite ideas about the authentic southern cooking they wanted to present, the Colletts opened the Old Portland Post Office Cafe. Although Tim had been involved in restaurants for eight years prior to opening their cafe, he claims to have learned his considerable cooking skills from his mother, a native of North Carolina.

"After some time in Europe, we had got used to the honest, good feelings we found in cafes and tavernas, and we wanted to promote those same feelings in our place here in Portland. We wanted to expand the cafe concept, to let people know that 'cafe' could mean more than just a greasy spoon serving burgers and fries."

The building housing the Old Portland Post Office Cafe has been a focal point in the historical development of the Northwest Portland Community since the 1890's. Only three other businesses have occupied the corner in 80 years: the Stanley Drug Company, Buckman Pharmacy and, for the past twenty-eight years, the Post Office Pharmacy and Fountain, so named for its proximity to the old Portland Post Office (now the U.S. Federal Building.) "We intend to continue the tradition of community service that has been a trademark of this location for so many years," say the Colletts, "and to combine it with the hospitality and warmth of Southern cooking. We depend a great deal upon the inspired help of our good friend and chef, Gregg Lindsey."

439 NW Broadway

Mint Julep

"They say you may always know the grave of a Virginian from the quantity of juleps he has drunk, as mint invariably springs up from where he has been buried."—Frederick Marryat, 1839

For each **Mint Julep:**

2 sprigs tender mint shoots
2 lumps sugar
¼ cup water
Crushed ice
2 to 3 ounces Sour Mash Whiskey
Garnish: fresh mint leaves
         powdered sugar

1. Using a tall glass for each mint julep, crush mint sprigs in the glass until most of the mint essence has been extracted. Remove mint.
2. In a small bowl, dissolve sugar lumps in water and set aside.
3. Fill julep glass with crushed ice.
4. Pour Sour Mash Whiskey over ice and allow it to become thoroughly chilled.
5. Add the sugar and water mixture.
6. Let the glass stand a few moments without stirring.
7. Dip fresh mint leaves in powdered sugar, garnish julep and serve immediately.

Iced Mint Tea

4 cups very strong tea
Juice of 6 oranges
1½ cups sugar
½ cup water
Zest of 1 orange
Several crushed mint leaves
Garnish: orange slices
       fresh mint sprigs

1. Combine strong tea with freshly squeezed orange juice. Set aside.
2. Boil sugar, water and orange zest in a saucepan 5 minutes.
3. Remove mixture from heat and add crushed mint leaves. Set aside to cool.
4. Half fill each of 6 iced tea glasses with crushed ice.
5. Add tea and orange juice mixture, and sweeten to taste with cooled mint syrup mixture.
6. Garnish each glass with an orange slice and sprig of mint.

Fresh Spinach Salad with Cafe House Dressing

Cafe House Dressing *is best if allowed to sit a day before it is used.*

2 bunches spinach
3 hard-cooked eggs
¼ to ½ pound fresh mushrooms, thinly sliced
3 strips bacon
⅓ cup finely chopped sweet onion
Cafe House Dressing

1. Wash, dry and tear spinach into a large salad bowl.
2. Peel and slice hard-cooked eggs.
3. Fry bacon until crisp. Drain, and break into bits.
4. Top spinach leaves with eggs and mushroom slices, crumbled bacon and onion.
7. Serve with **Cafe House Dressing.**

CAFE HOUSE DRESSING

1 teaspoon fines herbes
½ teaspoon granulated garlic
½ teaspoon salt
½ teaspoon black pepper
¾ teaspoon paprika
2 tablespoons molasses
2 dashes Lea and Perrins
1 cup salad oil
½ cup red wine vinegar

1. Mix all dry ingredients.
2. Add molasses and Lea and Perrins. Mix.
3. Add oil and wine vinegar; mix well.

Charleston Corn Soup

½ cup diced bacon
½ cup diced ham
1 tablespoon butter
1 onion, chopped
4 stalks celery, chopped
5 carrots, sliced
1 cup white wine
1 teaspoon oregano
½ teaspoon granulated garlic
½ teaspoon salt
1 tablespoon chicken stock base
Pinch cayenne
2 bay leaves
1 potato, peeled and sliced julienne
1 16-ounce can corn
⅓ cup finely chopped fresh parsley
2 quarts water

1. In a 3-quart saucepan, sauté bacon and ham. Add butter.
2. Stir in onion, celery and carrots.
3. Add wine and cook until onions become transparent.
4. Lower heat under pan and add oregano, garlic, salt, chicken stock base, cayenne and bay leaves. Slowly simmer 5 minutes.
5. Add potato, corn, fresh parsley and water. Let soup boil gently until potatoes are tender.

Oyster Pan Roast

"Has anyone (Southerners) ever dealt more triumphantly with the oyster and crab? Think of Southern-fried oysters, pickled oysters, oysters farcis, pan broiled oysters, scalloped oysters, oysters wrapped in bacon (little pigs in a blanket)..."
—*Old Dixie Southern Cookbook, 1839*

½ cup flour
½ cup cornmeal
1 teaspoon granulated garlic
½ teaspoon salt
¼ teaspoon pepper
½ cup butter
2 tablespoons tomato sauce
1 teaspoon Lea and Perrins
¼ teaspoon lemon juice
1 pint oysters, petite or extra small
Garnish: fresh fruit

1. Combine flour, cornmeal, granulated garlic, salt and pepper in a bowl. Set aside.
2. In a sauté pan over medium heat, combine butter, tomato sauce, Lea and Perrins and lemon juice.
3. Lightly bread oysters in cornmeal mixture.
4. Add breaded oysters to hot mixture in sauté pan; cook on each side until plump, about 1 to 2 minutes.
5. Serve on a bed of white rice, garnished with fresh fruit.

Southern Candied Tomatoes

2 16-ounce cans stewed tomatoes
1 teaspoon granulated garlic
½ teaspoon salt
½ teaspoon freshly ground pepper
2 tablespoons brown sugar
3 dashes Lea and Perrins
1 tablespoon flour
Croutons
¼ to ½ cup freshly grated Parmesan cheese

1. Preheat oven to 350 degrees.
2. Place tomatoes, garlic, salt, pepper, brown sugar, Lea and Perrins and flour into a large bowl. Mix ingredients together thoroughly.
3. Pour into a well buttered baking dish.
4. Top with **Croutons** and sprinkle with Parmesan.
5. Bake 30 to 45 minutes.

CROUTONS

4 slices toast
Butter
Powdered garlic

Butter each piece of toast evenly and sprinkle with powdered garlic. Cut into small squares.

Carolyn's Blueberry Pudding with Lemon Wine Sauce

½ cup flour
2 teaspoons baking powder
1 cup sugar
1 quart blueberries
1 egg, beaten
1 tablespoon butter, melted
Lemon Wine Sauce

1. Preheat oven to 300 degrees.
2. Sift flour, baking powder and sugar onto blueberries.
3. Add egg and butter.
4. Mix thoroughly, being careful not to mash berries.
5. Place mixture in cake pan; bake 45 minutes to 1 hour.
6. Spoon pudding into individual serving dishes and top with **Lemon Wine Sauce.**

LEMON WINE SAUCE

1 cup sugar
1 tablespoon flour
Juice of 1 lemon
½ cup water
½ cup dry red wine
1 tablespoon butter

Mix all ingredients together thoroughly in a saucepan and bring to a boil. Turn heat down immediately. Simmer the sauce 10 to 15 minutes.

This pudding can be served either hot or cold. It's especially nice with a cup of hot chicory coffee.

Pettygrove House

Dinner for Six

Mousse of Chicken Livers

*Suprême of Pacific Sole with Leek
and Red Wine Sauce*

Roast Squab with Thyme

*Meringue Gâteau with Strawberries
and Crème Chantilly*

Wines:

*With Mousse—Sokol Blosser Gewurztraminer, '78
With Sole—Hillcrest White Riesling, '77
With Squab—Eyrie Vineyards Pinot Noir, '76
With Gâteau—Château "R" Sauternes, '77*

*Benjamin Miles, Owner
Martin Kay, Chef*

A lovely old Victorian house in northeast Portland, built in 1893, has operated for some years now as a romantic little restaurant, serving set multi-course meals with choice of entrées. The familiar format has been retained by new owner Benjamin Miles and his chef, Martin Kay, while they are pouring new life and innovation into the restaurant's operation. Renovations on the house are ongoing, always with an eye toward maintaining the charm and craftsmanship of its period.

Miles, who came to the restaurant business from a career in precious metals, brought with him a passion for dining out, and dining well. Having frequently wearied of the menus in restaurants he patronized, he determined to change *his* menu often, and to feature interesting local products as well as delicacies from farther afield—always in their peak seasons. He applies his business and organizational skills to the accomplishment of these goals.

Chef Kay, a young Englishman whose culinary background includes the George V in Paris, five years apprenticeship at the Savoy Hotel in London, and further experience at the Hyde Park Hotel, came to Portland three years ago. He worked at the Polish Princess and The Woodstove before joining Miles at the Pettygrove House. Classical and hotel training and a motivation towards *nouvelle cuisine*—plus rampant creativity—make his cooking something to watch. Look for intriguing combinations, masterful sauces from fresh-made stocks, and captivating presentation. The multiple-course format provides a tiny taste of each of several of his creations on a given night...a perfect arrangement.

Benjamin Miles' ambitions for Pettygrove House are exciting news for Portland diners. With atmosphere and service being ever refined, and a fine wine cellar being assembled, this is a project worth following.

2287 NW Pettygrove

Mousse of Chicken Livers

12 ounces chicken livers
2 tablespoons olive oil
4 ounces butter, melted
6 ounces heavy cream
1 sprig lemon thyme
Salt and pepper
Parsley
Truffles—optional
6 slices hot toast

1. Dry livers on paper towels.
2. Sauté in olive oil and 2 tablespoons butter until just pink. Drain.
3. Pass through sieve or food processor. Beat in cream slowly until well incorporated. Add remaining butter, lemon thyme and salt and pepper to taste.
5. Chill in the refrigerator about 2 hours.
6. Chop parsley and truffle very finely. Take a scoop of mousse and coat it with this mixture and form into a small cake.
7. Serve on a doily with hot toast.

Sorbet of Tomato and Orange

1 onion, finely diced
3 tablespoons olive oil
6 ripe tomatoes, peeled and seeded
2 cloves garlic, crushed
1 sprig thyme
Salt and pepper
Zest of 1 orange, thinly pared and cut in fine julienne
6 sprigs fresh mint

1. Gently sweat onion in olive oil until transparent. Add tomatoes, garlic, thyme, salt and pepper.
2. Cook mixture until it loses its shape and resembles a pulp.
3. Put through a fine sieve; reserve.
4. Blanch orange zest in boiling water 10 seconds. Refresh in cold water.
5. Combine orange zest with tomato mixture and turn into an ice cream freezer. Crank until set.
6. Store in freezer until required. Serve in small crystal glasses with a sprig of mint in each.

Suprêmes of Pacific Sole with Leeks and Red Wine Sauce

24 ounces sole—4 ounces per serving
Seasoned fish stock to cover (fumet)
6 ounces leeks, washed and trimmed
Scant amount butter
Salt and black pepper
6 ounces red wine
2 to 3 ounces unsalted butter
6 ounces fish glaze—optional
Garnish: parsley—optional

1. Fold each portion of sole into a suprême (single fold).
2. Place in pan and add enough stock to cover. After covering with a tight-fitting lid, bring slowly to a boil. Remove from heat, leaving covered 2 to 3 minutes to finish cooking. Uncover and set aside, keeping fish slightly warm.
3. Thinly slice leeks, using only white and lightest green parts.
4. Sauté in scantest possible amount of butter. Season with salt and—generously—black pepper.
5. To assemble, gently pat leeks to absorb any remaining butter, then lay on serving plate. Drain fish and lay over leeks. At serving time, reduce fumet with red wine; when reduction will coat the back of a spoon, whip butter into it for thickening effect and, if desired, fish glaze.

Fish glaze is simply a fish stock which has been highly reduced, almost to a jelly. If you cannot find a commercial glaze, then you can make your own by the method described above.

If parsley is used as garnish, it should be done sparingly so as not to overwhelm.

Roast Squab with Thyme

6 squab—9 to 10 ounces per person
Salt and pepper
6 sprigs thyme
36 juniper berries, crushed
4 ounces butter, melted
2 ounces game glaze, i.e., completely reduced stock from a game bird or animal, or substitute chicken glaze

1. Preheat oven to 400 degrees.
2. Truss birds, seasoning inside and out with salt and pepper. Place thyme inside each with 6 juniper berries.
3. Roast 20 to 25 minutes, basting frequently with butter. When still slightly pink, remove from oven and keep warm.
4. Add game glaze to roasting pan. Reduce over heat, scraping up residue. Strain and serve with birds.

A carrot purée and wild rice would be nice accompaniments.

Juniper berries are available in most shops that carry specialty spices.

Meringue Gâteau with Strawberries and Crème Chantilly

8 egg whites
16 ounces sugar
Pinch salt
8 ounces strawberries
1 quart whipping cream
4 ounces confectioner's sugar
Vanilla extract
Crystallized violets

1. Preheat oven to lowest setting.
2. Ensure all equipment used for making meringue is clean and free of grease.
3. Whip white with half of sugar and a pinch of salt until very stiff. Fold in remaining sugar carefully.
4. Cut several 8" circles of wax paper. Flour paper, then pipe or spread meringue onto circles, filling as many as quantity allows.
5. Bake 1½ hours or until firm. Remove from paper as soon as possible and cool on racks.
6. Wash and hull strawberries; slice, reserving a few whole for garnish.
7. Whip cream with confectioner's sugar and vanilla until stiff.
8. Sandwich together layers of meringue with cream and strawberries. Decorate sides and top of cake with remaining cream and whole berries. Sprinkle crystallized violets over cake and serve well chilled.

TIP: Do not keep cake more than 24 hours.

Crystallized violets may be purchased at most gourmet food stores.

SEÑOR KORTE

Dinner for Four

Posole Stew

Sopaipillas

Chili Rellenos con Queso

Carne Adovada

Biscochitos

Beverages:

*Dos Equis or Tecate—
Imported Mexican Beers*

Señor Korte, Chef

One can grasp a true Mexican atmosphere in Portland any time by dining at the Señor Korte Restaurante. Examples of Mexican folk art and a handsome mural by Vernon Witham make for an authentic atmosphere. On a warm summer's evening, there is a patio with imported Mexican doors; a view of the red-tiled roof and the faint sound of marimba music almost convince the diner that he truly is in Mexico.

Señor Korte Restaurante specializes in New Mexican style cooking, a unique blend of Spanish and Pueblo Indian cuisine. Señor Korte, himself, has been cooking since he was five years old. This family has its own cookbook of "secret" recipes. Normally, the New Mexican style of cooking is hotter than most other Mexican cuisine. Señor Korte has, however, come up with a happy medium—allowing the Portland diner to eat authentically without a fire extinguisher at hand! The restaurant uses only fresh chilies sent from Santa Fe and prepares its sauces daily.

Vive Señor!

225 SW Ash

Posole Stew

2 pounds lean pork, cubed
1 quart water for cooking
1 teaspoon salt for water
2 to 3 pounds posole (or chicos)
4 garlic cloves, minced
½ teaspoon oregano
3 red chili pods, chopped, or 2 tablespoons chili powder

1. Boil pork in salted water until tender.
2. Add the posole (or chicos), garlic, oregano and chili pods; simmer in a heavy, covered pot until hominy kernels are bursting and soft.

This is excellent either served by itself or as a side dish.

Sopaipillas

4 cups sifted flour
1½ teaspoons salt
1 tablespoon baking powder
1 tablespoon shortening
1½ cups scalded milk, approximately

1. Combine dry ingredients and cut in shortening.
2. Add scalded milk to dry ingredients and work into dough, adding just enough to make a firm dough.
3. Knead 15 to 20 times; set aside for 10 minutes.
4. Roll dough to ⅛" thickness and cut into squares or triangles.
5. Fry the **Sopaipillas** in very hot fat (420 degrees). Keep reserved cut dough covered with a towel. Fry only a few at a time, and drain on absorbent toweling.

Serve as a bread with any southwestern meal. Deep fry in hot oil until golden brown.

Chili Rellenos con Queso

12 long slender green chilies
1 pound Cheddar cheese, cut in slices, then strips
1½ cups all purpose flour
1 teaspoon salt
Pepper to taste
1 cup milk
1 tablespoon oil
2 eggs, slightly beaten
Oil for frying

1. Peel the chilies; open a small slit below the stems and remove seeds.
2. Stuff with strips of cheese.
3. Mix the flour, salt and pepper. Blend the milk, oil and eggs.
4. Combine the two mixtures and stir only enough to mix.
5. Let batter stand 2 hours covered.
6. Roll stuffed chilies in batter. Deep fry in hot oil until golden brown.

These are excellent served with chili sauce and Spanish rice.

Carne Adovada
Marinated Pork

8 red chili pods
2 cups boiling water
¼ cup chopped onion
2 garlic cloves
1 teaspoon oregano
1 teaspoon salt
2½ pounds lean pork, cut in strips
Oil for frying

1. Remove stems, seeds and veins from the chilies. Wash them in warm water and put them in a pan; cover with the boiling water.
2. Let the chilies stand for an hour, or until the pulp separates easily from the skins.
3. Put through a food mill or colander, adding enough of the water the pods were cooked in to remove the pulp.
4. If sauce is too thick, thin with water. Add onion, garlic, oregano and salt. Mix well.
5. Marinate pork strips in the sauce for 24 hours.
6. To cook, cut pork strips into bite-size pieces. Heat enough oil in pan to keep strips from sticking. "Fry," covered with some chili sauce, until done; they should be nearly dried out. Strips may also be put in a baking dish in a 350 degree oven for 1 hour.

Biscochitos
Cookies

1 pound pure lard
1½ cups sugar
1 small glass wine or brandy
2 teaspoons anise seeds
6 cups flour
3 teaspoons baking powder
1 teaspoon salt
½ cup sugar blended with 1 teaspoon cinnamon

1. Cream shortening. Add sugar and cream well.
2. Add eggs and anise. Cream again.
3. Add wine.
4. Sift dry ingredients. Add to shortening mixture.
5. Roll out on floured board, thin.
6. Cut into shapes and sprinkle with cinnamon sugar mixture.
7. Bake in moderate oven for 10 to 15 minutes.

Dinner for Six

Silver Garden Ratatouille

German Onion Soup

Chicken Mendoza

Chef's Vegetables

Nüsstorte

Wines:

With Ratatouille—Preston Gewurztraminer, '77
With Chicken—Burgess Cellars Chardonnay, '77
With Nusstorte—Suduiraut Sauternes, '71

William Allen, Gail Schoelz and Norman Willis, Owners
Karl Krause, Chef

Purchased in California in 1977 by three restaurant-oriented entrepreneurs (for one-twentieth its original value!), and ushered from Los Angeles into Portland as a two-day movable feast for the new owners' friends, this former Amtrak domecar was then hoisted onto its present site beside the rails just east of the Willamette. An auxiliary kitchen and entrance were grafted on, and co-owner Gail Schoelz transformed the interior with dark greens, patterned carpets, metal and etched glass by Roger Ostrom.

Manager and co-owner Bill Allen says the scope of their project grew as the staff was assembled—visions of an "excellent prime rib house" metamorphosed into a more formal, "white tablecloth" restaurant with a broader menu range in order to give full sway to chef Karl Krause's expertise. Karl's training at the Culinary Institute of America and experience at the Benson Hotel, the Sun Valley Lodge, and several years as executive chef at Sun River, bear fruit at this smaller, yet quality operation. Everything is made from scratch, and the entire staff is dedicated to that sort of quality. Bill rejects the frequent suggestion that they add another car: "Our philosophy is to stay small, to try to do things with excellence. We're not interested in running people through here like sheep or cattle. We *could* serve more people, but no one on the staff would feel comfortable with that."

With an eye to de-mystifying wine selection, a well-organized range of regions, varieties, vintages and prices is offered. "People have been intimidated...we'd like to make it easy for people to begin to enjoy fine wines with confidence."

"We think we can induce people to come here—and to keep coming back—with that great triumvirate: good food, good wine, and atmosphere."

210 SE Ash

Silver Garden Ratatouille

2 medium zucchini
1 large onion
2 medium green peppers
1 medium eggplant
1 cup olive oil
3 cloves garlic
1 cup canned diced tomatoes
½ cup tomato purée
1 teaspoon sweet basil
1 teaspoon thyme
1 teaspoon oregano
Salt and pepper

1. Cut zucchini in half-wheels ³/₈" thick. Cut onion in ¹/₈" dice, and green pepper in ³/₈" dice.
2. Heat ⅔ of olive oil in thick-bottomed soup pot. Add zucchini and onion. Cook 5 minutes and add green peppers and garlic. Stir well.
3. In another pot heat remaining olive oil. Add eggplant dice and cook, stirring constantly, 5 minutes.
4. Add tomato purée, sweet basil, thyme and oregano, stirring to blend thoroughly.
5. Add eggplant and tomato mixture to other vegetables and simmer 10 minutes.
6. Season to taste with salt and pepper.

The **Ratatouille** *may be served immediately as a vegetable, or chilled and served as a salad. At the Silver Garden we serve it chilled on a leaf of butter lettuce, garnished with parsley.*

German Onion Soup

¼ pound bacon, diced
4 medium onions, sliced
3 ounces cabbage, shredded
4 ounces celery, sliced thin
2 ounces flour—optional
1 quart each beef and chicken stock, hot
2 tablespoons cider vinegar
¼ cup sherry
3 good shakes Worcestershire
Salt and pepper to taste

1. Sauté bacon in a soup pot.
2. Add onions to bacon drippings in soup pot and sauté until a light brown.
3. Add celery and cabbage. Continue cooking and stirring until all ingredients are cooked and browned.
4. Lower heat; add flour if desired, stirring continuously until flour is cooked, about 5 minutes.
5. Add hot beef and chicken stocks and stir vigorously until smooth and slightly thickened.
6. Add vinegar, sherry and Worcestershire; simmer 30 minutes.
7. Adjust seasoning with salt and pepper and serve.

Chicken Mendoza

⅓ pound butter
6 7-ounce whole boneless, skinless chicken breasts
3 ounces Cheddar cheese, grated
3 ounces Swiss cheese, grated
1 teaspoon oregano
1 teaspoon thyme
Dash salt and white pepper
Flour for dredging
2 eggs
¼ cup milk
Breadcrumbs
¼ cup clarified butter
Madeira Sauce
Béarnaise Sauce

1. Allow butter to soften at room temperature.
2. Flatten chicken breasts with a mallet to uniform thickness.
3. When butter is soft, add cheeses and herbs and blend well. Place in equally divided portions in center of each breast.
4. Fold each chicken breast around its mixture into a rectangular shape; pound edges together. Refrigerate until butter becomes firm.
5. Combine eggs and milk to make an eggwash. Dredge chicken packets in flour, transfer to eggwash, then to breadcrumbs. Season with salt and pepper.
6. Preheat oven to 375 degrees.
7. Heat clarified butter in a skillet and add chicken packets, frying until golden brown on both sides. Place immediately in preheated oven and bake 10 minutes.
8. Top with **Madeira Sauce** and a dollop of **Béarnaise Sauce.**
9. Serve with a rice pilaf and **Chef's Vegetables.**

Our waiters warn customers that when they first poke their knife or fork into the chicken, it may squirt. Beware!

MADEIRA SAUCE

½ cup Madeira
1 tablespoon minced shallots
1 teaspoon crushed peppercorns
2 cups brown sauce

1. Reduce Madeira, shallots and peppercorns over medium heat to ½ volume.
2. Strain into brown sauce. Stir and simmer 5 minutes.

BEARNAISE SAUCE

2 ounces minced shallots
1¼ teaspoons crushed peppercorns
1 cup tarragon vinegar
3 ounces cider vinegar
6 egg yolks
¼ cup cold water
1 pound butter, clarified
¾ teaspoon salt
⅛ teaspoon cayenne pepper
1 teaspoon finely chopped tarragon leaves—parsley may be substituted

1. Place shallots, 1 teaspoon peppercorns and tarragon vinegar in small saucepan. Reduce slowly until vinegar is nearly evaporated. Do not scorch.
2. Place residue in cheesecloth. Press or squeeze all liquid into small bowl and reserve.
3. Place remaining peppercorns in saucepan with cider vinegar. Boil and reduce. Cool.
4. Add egg yolks and water, and beat vigorously with whip. Place saucepan in bain-marie or large saucepan with boiling water—do not use double boiler. Continue to whip until mixture foams up and thickens to soft peak. When substance is like cooked soft custard, remove.
5. Begin to whip in clarified butter, adding it slowly with a ladle. Season with salt and cayenne pepper.
6. Add reserved liquid. Strain through cheesecloth and reserve in a warm place for immediate use. Makes 1½ quarts sauce.

Chef's Vegetables

2 zucchini, halved and sliced diagonally
3 celery stalks, sliced diagonally
2 carrots, halved and sliced diagonally
1 medium onion, sliced
1 ounce butter
¼ cup white wine
¼ cup lemon juice
Salt and pepper to taste

Sauté vegetables in butter until al dente. Add seasoning and finish with wine and lemon juice.

Nusstorte

This is a recipe from my Hungarian mother.

10 eggs
1 cup powdered sugar
2 cups finely grated walnuts
2 tablespoons rum
Butter
Flour
Frosting

1. Preheat oven to 350 degrees.
2. Separate eggs into large bowls. Add powdered sugar to egg yolks. Beat at high speed until thick and lemon yellow colored.
3. Using fresh beaters, beat whites until thick but not dry.
4. Add nuts and rum to yolks and mix thoroughly.
5. Fold mixtures together; pour into 10" springform pans which have had bottoms, but not sides, buttered and floured.
6. Bake 30 minutes in preheated oven. Cool.
7. Carefully slice through each layer to make 4 layers in all. Spread **Frosting** between layers and on top and side of cake.

FROSTING

½ pound unsalted butter
2 eggs
6 tablespoons granulated sugar
3 tablespoons cocoa

Combine all ingredients. Beat at high speed until light in color.

Dinner for Six

Camphor Wood and Tea Smoked Duck
(Szechuan)

Sliced Beef with Orange Peel in Hot Sauce
(Szechuan)

General Tso's Chicken
(Hunan)

Shanghai-Style Sweet and Pungent Pork

Wines:

With Duck—Gewurztraminer
With Beef—Eyrie Sauvignon Blanc
With Chicken—Sancerre
With Pork—Monmousseau Rose d'Anjou

Paul Anderson, Owner
Chi-Siung Chen, Chef

Uncle Chen's is a new and exciting concept in a Chinese restaurant for the Pacific Northwest, offering the wealth and variety of the many styles of this oldest of cuisines as well as a concern for the total ambiance.

Designer Carol Edelman and textile designer Larry Kirkland have created a spacious, light-colored dining room magnificently accented with brightly colored Chinese banners. White linen, bentwood chairs and fresh flowers add a formal air to this transformed old Third Avenue building. Perhaps the most intriguing area of the restaurant is the glass-covered courtyard hung with colorful, flamboyant Chinese kites and surrounded by six-story buildings—a "New York alley turned elegant!"

The *raison d'etre* for this unusual restaurant is a young man of uncommon talent and experience, "Uncle" Chi-Siung Chen. "Uncle" translates to "master", and Chen is master indeed of the six Chinese cuisines featured at his restaurant. Born in a province near Shanghai and apprenticed at age fifteen, Chen later worked for some time under a famous Fukien chef, then in a Taiwan restaurant featuring many styles, where he gained experience in Canton and Peking cuisines. Emigrating to New York in 1973, he was hired by Peng's. There he learned—from Peng, who had previously cooked for Chiang Kai-shek, and whose restaurant has been rated by Gourmet magazine as the finest in the city—the spicy Hunan and Szechuan cuisines. Before leaving Peng's, Chen had advanced to head chef, becoming well-qualified to offer his talents in his own unique setting in the Pacific Northwest.

529 SW 3rd

This meal is constructed like a special Chinese banquet with all meat and poultry dishes. The simple vegetable dishes Westerners think of as so typically Chinese are omitted in favor of the more extravagant meat dishes for a special occasion.

Camphor Wood and Tea Smoked Duck

3 teaspoons salt
1 teaspoon Szechuan peppercorns
1 star anise
1 teaspoon saltpeter
1 4-to-5 pound duckling
¼ cup camphor wood scraps or, if not available, other wood scraps
2 teaspoons black tea leaves
8 cups oil for frying
Dipping Sauce
24 2" sections green onion

1. Heat pan and stir-fry salt over medium heat until lightly brown.
2. Add peppercorns, anise and saltpeter; stir-fry until fragrant. Remove and set aside until cool enough to handle.
3. Rub interior and exterior of duckling thoroughly with salt mixture and allow to sit 6 hours or overnight. Rinse duckling lightly and drain.
4. Place on a rack in heatproof pan with water in bottom; steam 40 minutes over high heat.
5. Preheat oven to 450 degrees.
6. Place wood scraps and tea leaves in pan on lower shelf of oven. Place duckling on rack directly above and bake 5 minutes or until outside is golden brown. Remove.
7. Heat oil for deep-frying to 380 degrees. Fry duckling 8 minutes or until skin is crispy. Remove and drain. Cut into bite-size pieces and serve with **Dipping Sauce** and green onions.

DIPPING SAUCE

4 teaspoons oil
2 teaspoons sweet bean paste (Tan Min Chun)
2 teaspoons sugar
2 teaspoons water

Heat oil. Stir-fry all ingredients until boiling.

Sliced Beef with Orange Peel in Hot Sauce

1 pound beef tenderloin
5 cups oil
4 dried red peppers
10 Szechuan peppercorns
1 star anise
2 teaspoons soy sauce
⅓ teaspoon salt
2 teaspoons sugar
1 cup water
1 teaspoon sesame oil
Peel of 1 orange, shredded

1. Cut beef into slices ⅓" thick.
2. Heat oil for deep-frying. Fry beef slices about 8 minutes; drain.
3. Pour off all but 3 cups oil. Stir-fry red pepper, peppercorns and anise. Add remaining ingredients with beef and cook about 8 minutes over medium heat until thickened.

TIP: This dish may also be made with chicken.

General Tso's Chicken

6 chicken legs
1 egg
1 cup cornstarch
7 cups oil
1¼ teaspoons salt
1¼ teaspoons pepper
8 dried red peppers
3 green onions, chopped
2 teaspoons minced garlic
Sauce

1. Remove skin from chicken legs. Cut in 1¼" pieces through the bone.
2. Combine egg, cornstarch, 1 cup oil, salt and pepper. Marinate chicken in this mixture 30 minutes.
3. Heat remaining 6 cups oil to 375 degrees. Deep-fry chicken 5 minutes and drain.
4. Heat a little of the oil and stir-fry red peppers, green onions and garlic with the chicken and **Sauce** 1 minute. Serve.

SAUCE

1 teaspoon minced ginger
1 teaspoon sesame oil
½ teaspoon cornstarch
1 cup water
1 cup vinegar
1 cup soy sauce
½ cup hot oil

Combine all ingredients.

Shanghai-Style Sweet and Pungent Pork

This dish is very different from the sweet and sour pork usually found in Chinese restaurants.

⅔ pound pork loin
1 teaspoon soy sauce
1 egg yolk
8½ teaspoons cornstarch
1 small green pepper
6 cups vegetable oil
½ teaspoon chopped garlic
1 cup **Pickled Vegetable Salad**
3 teaspoons vinegar
3 teaspoons sugar
4½ teaspoons water
3 teaspoons tomato ketchup
⅓ teaspoon salt

1. Remove any fat or tough membrane from pork loin. Cut pork into slices ⅔" thick. Using blunt edge of cleaver, lightly pound to tenderize. Cut slices into bite-size pieces.
2. Mix pork with mixture of soy sauce, egg yolk, and 1 teaspoon cornstarch and let marinate 20 minutes. Mix with 6 teaspoons cornstarch.
3. Remove seeds from green pepper and cut into bite-size pieces.
4. Heat oil for deep-frying to about 375 degrees. Fry pork pieces 3 minutes. Remove and reheat oil to 400 degrees. Refry pork pieces another 30 seconds. Remove and drain.
5. Reheat pan with 3 teaspoons oil. Stir-fry chopped garlic until fragrant. Add green pepper and **Pickled Vegetable Salad.** Stir-fry briefly.
6. Add vinegar, sugar, 3 teaspoons water, ketchup and salt. Combine 1½ teaspoons each water and cornstarch and add when mixture has come to a boil, stirring constantly.
7. Add fried pork pieces and toss lightly to mix. Serve immediately.

PICKLED VEGETABLE SALAD

1 cucumber
1 large turnip
2 large carrots
2 slices ginger root
1 cup white wine vinegar

1. Peel vegetables and cut in small cubes or in julienne strips.
2. Heat wine vinegar to a boil and stir in sugar to dissolve.
3. Pour over vegetables and refrigerate, covered, overnight. Drain to use.

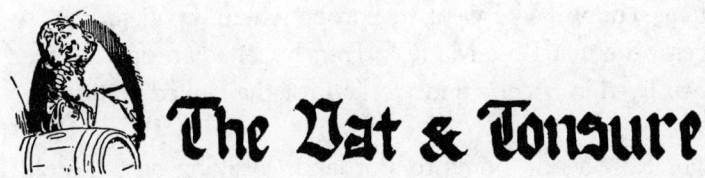

The Vat & Tonsure

Dinner for Six

Artichoke with Caper Mayonnaise

Fennel Pork Roast with Fresh Broccoli

Tomato Salad

Sour Cream Peach Pie

Beverages:
With Artichoke—Frascati Superiore Secco
With Pork Roast—Rüdesheimer Wiesberg, '76
With Peach Pie—Espresso

Mike and Rose-Marie Quinn, Owners
Rose-Marie Quinn, Cook

As a student at Portland State University in the sixties, Mike Quinn worked part-time as a waiter at The Gay Nineties restaurant on SW Park Avenue. Upon finishing school, Mike went to Europe where, in Vienna at—where else, the opera—he met Rose-Marie, a French-Canadian opera singer. For ten years they lived in Vienna and worked for the United Nations.

Mike brought Rose-Marie home to Portland. Walking past the old Gay Nineties one day and finding it not only closed but boarded-up, Mike was intrigued. Investigation proved the space was available for leasing; within several months the Quinns had opened the Vat and Tonsure.

"I don't in any way consider myself a chef," says Rose-Marie, who does all the cooking at the sign-of-the-monk. "but I have always enjoyed cooking. We offer good, wholesome food, using what is seasonally fresh."

825 SW Park

Artichoke with Caper Mayonnaise

Juice of ½ lemon
4 bay leaves
1 teaspoon dried basil
4 cups water
6 large artichokes
Lemon halves for rubbing
Caper Mayonnaise
Garnish: lemon wedges

1. Place lemon juice, bay leaves, basil and water in a large saucepan and bring to a boil.
2. Trim ends of artichoke leaves with kitchen shears.
3. Remove "choke" with a spoon by separating leaves with your fingers and scooping from inside.
4. Cut off artichoke stems, leaving flat bottoms.
5. Rub each artichoke all over with a lemon half.
6. Place artichokes in boiling water; cook 30 to 45 minutes, or until bottoms are easily pierced with a fork. Remove and set aside to cool.
7. Serve on individual plates with lemon wedges and small bowls of **Caper Mayonnaise.**

CAPER MAYONNAISE

1½ cups mayonnaise
Juice of ½ lemon
1½ tablespoons Dijon mustard
2 tablespoons capers
Freshly ground black pepper

Mix all ingredients thoroughly. Refrigerate.

Fennel Pork Roast with Fresh Broccoli

6 to 7 pounds lean pork loin, boned
5 large cloves garlic, pressed
1 tablespoon ground coriander
Salt and freshly ground black pepper
Leafy fennel sprigs (sweet anise)
2 tablespoons Pernod or Anisette
Broccoli

1. Preheat oven to 425 degrees.
2. Butterfly pork with a sharp knife, forming a rectangle 15" long and 10" wide. Remove excess back fat.
3. Combine pressed garlic and coriander to make a paste; rub onto surface of pork.
4. Salt and pepper surface liberally, and lay fennel sprigs across top.
5. Roll jellyroll-fashion; tie every 2" with kitchen twine.
6. Place in a shallow roasting pan; cook 1 hour in preheated oven.
7. Heat Pernod or Anisette in a saucepan. Ignite and pour over roast to flambé. Turn heat to 400 degrees.
8. Return roast to oven and cook 1 more hour. Remove and let rest 10 minutes.
9. Carve into ½" slices.
10. Baste with pan juices and serve with **Broccoli.**

TIP: The meat should be basted with pan juices every 15 minutes during cooking to retain its moisture.

BROCCOLI

1½ pounds broccoli flowers with 3" stems
Pinch salt
Pinch tarragon

1. Place broccoli in a large pan of boiling water.
2. Add salt and tarragon and cook 4 minutes, uncovered.
3. Remove from water and serve immediately.

TIP: This vegetable should be cooked just before serving the entrée.

Tomato Salad

6 medium tomatoes
Green olive oil
Juice of 1 lemon
Fresh basil leaves

1. Halve the tomatoes lengthwise and cut each half into 7 slices.
2. Fan 2 halves across each salad plate and sprinkle with green olive oil, lemon juice and basil leaves.

Sour Cream Peach Pie

PASTRY:

⅓ cup lard
¼ teaspoon salt
1 cup sifted unbleached flour
¼ cup chilled soda water

1. Work lard and salt into flour until it forms little lumps.
2. Add just enough soda water so the dough is pliable, not sticky—you may not need entire amount.
3. Shape into a ball and refrigerate 1 hour.
4. Roll out dough ⅛ thick and line a 10" pie plate. Chill until needed.

FILLING:

5 ripe peaches, thinly sliced
1 tablespoon peach brandy
2 eggs
1½ tablespoons sifted unbleached flour
¼ teaspoon salt
¼ cup sugar
2 cups sour cream
Topping

1. Preheat oven to 375 degrees.
2. Toss peach slices with peach brandy and set aside.
3. In a large bowl, beat eggs until frothy.
4. Add flour, salt and sugar and beat well. Mix in sour cream.
5. Carefully fold in sliced fruit and pour mixture into unbaked pie shell.
6. Bake 20 minutes, sprinkle with **Topping** and bake another 50 minutes.
7. Let pie cool and refrigerate at least 4 hours.

TOPPING:

½ cup butter
1 cup unbleached, all purpose flour
⅓ cup sugar

1. Cut butter into flour.
2. Add sugar and combine until mixture has fine grainy appearance. Set aside.

WINTERBORNE

Dinner for Six

Spinach Timbale with Sour Cream Sauce

Mediterranean Fish Soup

Scallops in Vermouth

Leaf Lettuce Salad with Vinaigrette

Stuffed Sole with Tart White Butter

Vegetables à la Juniper

Ice Cream with Peaches and Sauterne

Wines:

With Timbale—Trimbach Gewurztraminer
With Sole—Côte des Colombe Chenin Blanc

Dwight Bacon, Owner & Chef

Winterborne is a small, unique seafood restaurant with a very limited menu, wonderful specials, and an integrity of purpose and of execution that is truly gratifying. Owner and chef Dwight Bacon says, "We opened in autumn '77 after despairing of finding edible fish east of the river. We were determined to treat our seafood and our customers with equal care, dealing conscientiously with what we have and not promising more."

That is a succinct explanation of his style. Dwight spent some years out in the country living a very different manner and pace than city life offers. He cooked in a pottery workshop for fifty vegetarians, for short stints at several restaurants, and then for a longer period, at the Manzanita Inn on the coast. Making the jump back to city life, he consciously preserved his attachment to simplicity, honesty, and spontaneity in a restaurant world dedicated to the superficial, the packaged and the quick. The answer for him was to cook a few, fresh, local things well in an unpretentious, low-key, but tasteful atmosphere.

"Seafood lends itself to sauces," he observes, "and the French are good at sauces, so there is a French influence, but we like to understate things."

He is also very concerned that his food be digestible and healthful. "We make everything here and add nothing to it to prolong its life or shorten yours. We want our food to appeal to the eye, the nose and the palate, but not at the expense of digestion. We want a restaurant we aren't afraid to eat at."

Dwight would prefer to have no set menu, but to offer the best seafood available prepared in the way that would best suit it—and him—that day. As a compromise he offers a menu with a few set dishes and then several daily specials which showcase the freshest fish available and his greatest creativity.

The homemade bread, appetizers, soup and desserts which complement the seafood entrées are all of such a level of quality and tastiness as to leave the diner truly satisfied beyond his expectations—exactly Dwight's intention!

3520 NE 42nd

Spinach Timbale with Sour Cream Sauce

6 tablespoons butter, melted
1½ pounds fresh spinach
Fresh mint leaves
3 tablespoons flour
1 cup milk
3 eggs, beaten
1 shallot, minced
1 teaspoon salt
2 tablespoons lemon juice
Sour cream
Wine
Garnish: 6 orange slices
          mint leaves

1. Preheat oven to 375 degrees.
2. Grease 6 molds with 3 tablespoons melted butter and place in freezer.
3. Steam spinach in a little water with several fresh mint leaves until wilted. Remove, cool and squeeze out moisture.
4. Make roux with 3 tablespoons each butter and flour. Add milk and stir until thick.
5. Combine spinach and mint with roux, eggs, shallot, salt and lemon juice and blend well. Pour into prepared molds.
6. Place molds in baking pan and surround with 1" boiling water. Bake until firm and slightly puffed, about 15 to 20 minutes.
7. Serve hot or cold with sour cream seasoned with chopped mint and a little wine. Garnish with mint and orange slices.

Mediterranean Fish Soup

Fish stock or clam juice or both
Red Sauce
Fennel seed, chopped
Zest of orange
Canned chopped clams—optional

1. Heat stock.
2. Add **Red Sauce** to taste.
3. Gently bring to boil. Reduce heat to simmer. Add fennel and orange zest to taste and clams if using. Serve.

RED SAUCE

1 cup olive oil
½ to ¾ cup dried basil
10 medium-to-large onions, chopped
2 heads garlic, minced
3 #10 cans cored, whole tomatoes

1. Heat olive oil over very low heat in a stainless steel or enameled kettle. Add basil.
2. Add onions and garlic. Let this simmer slowly about 1 hour.
3. Chop tomatoes coarsely. Add approximately ½ can at a time to onions and garlic. Cook over low, even heat several hours. Cool overnight.
4. Return to heat next morning and cook 4 to 5 hours more. Remove from heat to cool slightly, then refrigerate until used.

Red Sauce *has many uses and keeps well. This recipe makes about one gallon.*

Scallops in Vermouth

TIP: Step 2 is crucial. Scallops should exude juices, but not be fully cooked. In fact, I don't think scallops should ever be fully cooked.

1½ pounds scallops
Very dry vermouth, chilled
Juice of 1 lemon
3 tablespoons shallots
1½ teaspoons tarragon
1 ounce butter
1 ounce flour
3 ounces cream
2 egg yolks
Breadcrumbs

1. Carefully wash scallops, and quarter. Add cold vermouth to cover. Add lemon juice, shallots and tarragon. Marinate 3 hours to overnight.
2. Heat scallops in heavy enameled pan, covered, over low heat until marinade is just hot to touch. Remove from heat and set aside, covered, 5 to 10 minutes. *See note above.*
3. Remove and reserve scallops, well drained. Reduce remaining marinade by ⅓ volume. Remove from heat and strain.
4. Cook butter and flour until raw smell of flour disappears. Add hot marinade and stir until smooth. Place over low heat 15 minutes, stirring occasionally. Add accumulated juices from reserved scallops.
5. Add cream and egg yolks, off heat. Stir to blend.
6. If not to be served immediately, stir sauce to cool slightly, add scallops and refrigerate.
7. To serve, place portions in scallop shells on baking sheet. Cover with breadcrumbs and heat in 400 degree oven until sauce begins to bubble.

Leaf Lettuce Salad with Vinaigrette

Butter lettuce
Salad Bowl or Oak Leaf lettuce
Red Leaf lettuce
Vinaigrette

1. Wash and drain lettuce. Tear into small pieces, and refrigerate.
2. Toss with **Vinaigrette** and serve.

VINAIGRETTE

Olive oil
White wine vinegar
Lemon juice
Garlic, minced
Scallions, white end and some green, thinly sliced
Salt and pepper
Dill, rosemary, thyme..."dealer's choice"

Mix olive oil, vinegar and lemon juice with garlic, scallions, salt and pepper and herbs to taste.

Proportions are intentionally omitted for **Vinaigrette** *because everyone has his own preference for proportions.*

Stuffed Sole with Tart White Butter

12 4-ounce filets petrale sole
½ pound roasted almonds, roughly chopped
1 shallot, minced
⅓ teaspoon lavender mint, crumbled
10 ounces baby shrimp
Szechuan peppercorns, ground
2 ounces butter, melted
Tart White Butter

1. Preheat oven to 400 degrees.
2. Wash and dry filets.
3. Combine almonds, shallot, mint and shrimp and chop together. Sprinkle with pepper and moisten with a little butter. Mix gently, but well.
4. Place one filet on bottom of buttered individual ovenware serving dish. Cover loosely with stuffing, top with another filet and brush with butter. Bake 8 to 10 minutes.
5. Cover with **Tart White Butter** and serve with **Vegetables à la Juniper.**

TART WHITE BUTTER

1 cup fine white wine vinegar
2 ounces Chablis
Juice of 1 lemon
2 shallots, minced
½ pound butter, frozen and cut into ¼" pieces
Salt

1. Combine vinegar, wine, lemon juice and shallots in saucepan. Reduce to consistency of marmalade. Off heat, beat in 2 pieces butter until melted.
2. Replace over low heat, gradually beating in remaining butter. Salt to taste.

TIP: We use Amora vinegar, which contains some lemon juice.

If sauce refuses to take the butter or breaks, add 1 or 2 tablespoons of cold water. This will test your luck.

The Côte des Columbe Chenin Blanc served at our restaurant with this dish is aged in Oregon oak at the winery in Banks, Oregon.

Vegetables à la Juniper

3 or more vegetables of the season, e.g., cauliflower, broccoli, carrots, turnips, rutabagas, zucchini, celery
4 quarts water
½ cup olive oil
1 teaspoon juniper berries
1 teaspoon peppercorns
3 bay leaves
1 teaspoon rosemary *or* ½ teaspoon thyme
Salt to taste
Vinegar to taste

1. Separate cauliflower and broccoli into flowerettes. Slice broccoli stems ¼" thick. Slice carrots, turnips and rutabagas about ⅛" thick. Halve zucchini lengthwise and cut into ½" pieces. Cut celery into ⅓" slices.
2. Bring water to rolling boil. Add oil and spices. Place a colander in the pan to aid in removing vegetables.
3. Add vegetables and cook according to this approximate timetable for order of entry and cooking times:
    cauliflower: 2 minutes
    sliced broccoli stems: 2 minutes
    celery: 1 minute
    zucchini: 45 seconds
    carrots: 40 seconds
    turnips: 30 seconds
    rutabagas: 30 seconds
    broccoli flowerettes: 15 seconds
3. Remove vegetables from water and toss with salt and vinegar. Serve a generous portion with **Stuffed Sole**.

Try to choose a mixture of colors and textures such as cauliflower with carrots and zucchini.

Juniper berries are a somewhat uncommon ingredient: it may be necessary to check at several gourmet food shops...or, go east of the Cascades and shake a tree, as do we!

Ice Cream with Peaches and Sauterne

4 ripe peaches
4 ounces sauterne
1 tablespoon lemon juice
1 quart vanilla ice cream

1. Peel peaches; if your peaches prefer to hang on to their skins, dip for 10 to 15 seconds in boiling water, then into cool water. Slice thinly.
2. Toss peaches with sauterne and lemon juice. Cover and set aside.
3. At serving time put a layer of peaches in bottom of dessert dish, then an appropriate portion of ice cream, then top with peaches, spooning liquid over top of all.

If your peaches lack flavor or if you have a fondness for spice, toss peaches and sauterne with sprinkles of cinnamon or freshly ground nutmeg, or—particularly—freshly ground coriander.

The quality of the ice cream is very important. If you are not fortunate enough to live near 44th and Fremont where Rose's makes the best in town, make your own.

Dinner for Six

*Quenelles Mousselines of Sole
with Coulis of Crayfish*

Fred's Bread

Soup Purée of Leek, Potato and Carrot

Breast of Duckling with Limes and Sesame

Rice Pilaf

A Light Green Salad

Boccone Dolce

Wines:

*With Quenelles—Rodet Puligny Montrachet, '76
With Duckling—Eyrie Vineyards Pinot Noir, 75*

*Paul Anderson, Owner
Fred Finger, Chef de Cuisine*

This interesting little building, formerly a cafe and a barber shop, was bought two years ago by Paul Anderson, who proceeded to staff it largely from his previous restaurant, the Polish Princess.

The atmosphere in this nearly hundred-year-old building has been lightened and modernized, yet retains many lovely old details: the large old fireplace, frequently used in cooking entrées, simple oak reproduction chairs and tables, and candles at each table, covered with lovely translucent glass bells. Tables in the bar—popular for appetizers and desserts as well—are beautiful, exposed-grain pedestals by Fred Enera. Small bouquets of fresh flowers accent the tables and garnish the dishes.

Chef Fred Finger, with one eye toward nouvelle cuisine and one toward health consciousness, presents a cuisine both novel and inventive, with a menu which changes daily. A native of Greenwich Village, Finger studied art and music before cooking with the late Michael Field, and carries over his inherent creativity to his culinary career. Learning his trade at several Oregon restaurants, including his own in Old Town, Fred's preferences have emerged: fresh local products, daily fresh baked breads, interesting combinations of ingredients and sauces that enhance rather than mask natural flavors. Herbs from The Woodstove's garden may blend with locally raised champignons de la foret, Oregon crayfish and other interesting products in dishes inspired by the cuisines of all the world.

A young, enthusiastic and committed dining room staff and a lovely well-rounded wine list complete the picture of this imaginative restaurant.

2601 NW Vaughn

Quenelles of Sole with Coulis of Crayfish

1 pound filet of sole
1 to 2 egg whites—the less used the better
2 teaspoons salt
½ teaspoon white pepper
½ teaspoon nutmeg
1 pint heavy cream or crème fraîche
Butter
Coulis of Crayfish
Garnish: crayfish tails

1. In a food processor purée sole with 1 egg white until well blended. Add seasonings and cream. Process until very smooth and light, yet with enough body to hold its shape in a spoon. If too light to do so, add another egg white, ½ at a time.
2. Poach a sample to taste for seasoning and texture. Season to taste if needed, or add more egg white or cream. Chill until needed.
3. Butter well the bottom of a skillet large enough to hold quenelles.
4. Select 2 equal-size spoons. Gently scoop up quenelle mixture with first. Dip the other in hot water; while it is still hot and moist, delicately "cup" the other spoon full of quenelle mixture, just enough to shape an oval. Handling with great care, repeat until the skillet has neat rows of quenelle forms, leaving room for expansion.
5. Gently "slide" lightly salted water down inner side of skillet until quenelles are covered. Bring slowly to simmer. Poach gently approximately 10 minutes or until done.
6. Drain and serve napped with **Coulis of Crayfish.** Pour a ribbon of the coulis around the quenelles and garnish plate with crayfish tails.

COULIS OF CRAYFISH

3 cups raw mirepoix (carrot, onion and celery cut in julienne)
¼ cup olive oil
¼ cup clarified butter
3 dozen live crayfish
3 ounces brandy, flamed
6 ounces white wine
6 ounces fumet (fish stock)
Bouquet garni of parsley, thyme, bay leaf
Salt to taste
1 pint veal glaze (rich veal stock reduced down to a glaze)
Approximately 1 pint water
½ pound butter
1 pint cream
Cayenne
Freshly squeezed lemon juice
Sweet paprika

1. Cook julienned vegetables in oil and butter.
2. Wash and clean crayfish. Gut them by pulling central tail flap. As they are gutted, toss them live into the tender mirepoix.
3. When all the critters are in the pot, add flamed brandy, wine, fumet, bouquet garni, and salt to taste. Bring to a boil; simmer 5 minutes.
4. Remove crayfish. Remove tails from crayfish and reserve. Return bodies to stock. Add veal glaze and cook 25 minutes more, reducing gently. Remove bouquet garni.
5. Purée in batches in food processor. Force through sieve, pressing hard to extract all flavor particles. Reserve and cool, skimming periodically.
6. Meanwhile, shell tails. Reserve shells and dry them in oven at 375 degrees until brittle.
7. Clean tails and refrigerate until needed.
8. Rinse sieve with the water; reserve water.
9. Grind shells with butter in food processor. Rinse processor with reserved water and add to butter.
10. Bring mixture to boil and simmer until it takes color of shells.
11. Strain through linen towel or several layers of cheesecloth and squeeze when cool to extract all flavor and color. Chill the mixture to raise the butter and collect it off the liquid. You should have about 6 ounces of intensively colored crayfish butter.
12. Strain cooled sauce from Step 5 into clean saucepan and reduce to 1 pint. Add cream and reduce by ¼.
13. Swirl in crayfish butter and tails and season to taste with salt, cayenne, lemon juice and paprika.

Fred's Bread

Makes 4 large loaves

4 cups slightly warm water
1 cup honey
¼ cup granulated yeast
6 to 7 cups unbleached white bread flour
¼ cup salt
1 cup sesame seeds
1 cup melted unsalted butter
6 to 7 cups whole wheat flour
Butter
Shortening to grease pans
Cornmeal

1. Combine water, honey, yeast, and 4 cups white flour until smooth. Proof until bubbling and swollen.
2. Add salt, sesame seeds, butter and 4 cups whole wheat flour and beat until well mixed. Knead in remaining flour alternately until dough is satiny and resilient to the touch.
3. Place in buttered bowl, spread lightly with butter and let rise in draft-free place till doubled. Punch down and let rise again.
4. Remove, cut into 4 sections and let rest 10 minutes while you preheat oven to 425 degrees and treat pans by greasing with shortening, then dusting well with cornmeal. Shape into loaves; butter tops and sprinkle with cornmeal. Cover loosely with a cloth. Let rise again until doubled.
5. Bake 10 minutes. Reduce heat to 375 degrees and bake 35 minutes or until done.
6. Remove from oven. Cool in pans 10 to 15 minutes. Remove to rack and let cool.

Soup Purée of Leek, Potato, and Carrot

2 cups sliced leeks
¼ pound unsalted butter
2 cups sliced potatoes
2 cups sliced carrots
2 quarts light stock or water
Bouquet garni with fresh mint sprig
Salt and pepper to taste
Mace to taste

1. Cook leeks gently in butter until very, very tender.
2. Add potatoes, carrots, and stock. Bring to a boil and skim. Add bouquet garni and simmer until vegetables are cooked to a pulp. Remove bouquet.
3. Purée through fine sieve. Season to taste. Serve hot.

You may also cool the soup and chill until very cold. Stir in one cup heavy cream and season again to taste. Cold soups should be highly seasoned.

Breast of Duckling with Limes and Sesame

⅔ cup white wine vinegar
½ cup sugar
Zests of 6 to 12 limes, cut in julienne
1 pint clear, reduced duck stock or veal stock
1 tablespoon potato starch
⅓ cup fresh lime juice (6 to 12 limes)
1 tablespoon dark rum
2 to 3 tablespoons lime marmalade—optional
2 to 3 tablespoons toasted sesame seeds
6 breasts of duckling, skin left on, trimmed
Salt and pepper
Fresh spinach leaves
6 limes, peeled and thinly sliced

1. Cook vinegar and sugar with julienned peel until mixture is a very pale caramel. Let cool.
2. Heat stock and bind with potato starch. Add to caramel to dissolve. Bring to a boil.
3. Add lime juice. Simmer gently 10 to 15 minutes until reduced to 1 pint. Add rum and marmalade. Reserve and keep warm.
4. Preheat broiler until rack is hot.
5. Pepper duck on both sides. Salt skin side only. Place, skin up, on rack above pans 6" from heat. Broil 5 minutes. Turn over. Baste once with drippings and broil 5 minutes. Give a quarter turn and broil 5 minutes. Turn over and broil 5 minutes more or until done.
6. Remove and let rest 5 minutes in a warm place on a pan to collect juices.
7. Arrange spinach attractively on 6 large dinner plates. Carve breasts into long, thin slices on a slight bias. Arrange as a fan across the spinach.
8. Add reserved juices to sauce, glaze duck, sprinkle with sesame seeds, and decorate breasts with a line of sliced limes.
9. Serve with **Rice Pilaf.**

TIP: Roasting time is approximate. Be sure not to overcook. Meat should still have some pink color.

RICE PILAF

¼ cup clarified butter
1 small onion, minced
1 cup rice
1½ cups chicken stock
Bay leaf
Sprig of thyme
Salt and pepper
Butter
Blanched almonds, sautéed—optional

1. Preheat oven to 350 degrees.
2. Sauté onion in butter until very tender. Increase heat and lightly brown.
3. Add rice and stir until coated and milky white.
4. Meanwhile, boil chicken stock. Add to pan along with bay leaf, thyme, salt and pepper. Stir once. Bring to a boil. Cover and bake 35 minutes or until all liquid is absorbed.
5. Allow rice to sit a minute, then toss with butter, almonds if desired, and any other seasonings desired, to taste.

A Light Green Salad

2 to 3 smallish heads butter lettuce
Vinaigrette
Garnish: a few capers
       mushrooms, trimmed and sliced

1. Separate lettuce leaves. Wash and dry.
2. Toss with **Vinaigrette** and garnish with capers and mushrooms.

VINAIGRETTE

1 tablespoon honey
1 tablespoon Pommery mustard
3 pints light olive oil, or 2 pints safflower oil with 1 pint olive oil
1 ounce white wine vinegar
Juice of ½ lemon
1 to 2 cloves garlic, puréed
Crushed sweet basil, to taste
Salt and freshly ground pepper

1. Combine honey and mustard.
2. Mix with all other ingredients.

Boccone Dolce

Meringue
1 pint fresh ripe strawberries
Chocolate Glaze
1 pint whipping cream
⅓ cup sugar
Vanilla extract to taste

1. Preheat oven to 200 degrees.
2. Prepare **Meringue.**
3. Meanwhile wash, hull, and slice strawberries, reserving 14 perfect berries.
4. Prepare **Chocolate Glaze.**
5. Spread **Chocolate Glaze** over top of 1 meringue layer and over bottoms of others. Let cool until set and firm.
6. Whip cream with sugar and vanilla until very stiff.
7. Spread a thin layer of cream evenly over layer with glazed top. Cover with half of sliced berries. Cover with next layer.
8. Spread this layer with cream, then with remaining sliced berries. Top with remaining layer.
9. Spread sides and top evenly with remaining cream, reserving some to pipe decoratively on top. Place 12 of the perfect berries in a pattern around the cake's rim. Place 1 berry in the center.
10. With a pastry bag, pipe cream on top as desired.
11. Chill cake briefly and serve.

Dip the last berry in what remains of the **Chocolate Glaze** *and in the last dab of cream, then on your tongue. Crush and absorb the flavors.*

MERINGUE

4 egg whites
1⅓ cups sugar
Pinch salt
⅛ teaspoon cream of tartar

1. Preheat oven to 200 degrees.
2. Beat all ingredients together until stiff.
3. Line baking pans with parchment and trace 3 10" circles on the paper.
4. Fill circles with meringue. Smooth tops, place in oven and bake until dry, approximately 1 hour.
5. Remove from oven and peel off paper. Cool on rack.

TIP: It helps to prop oven door ajar with a spoon if your heat is uneven.

CHOCOLATE GLAZE

6 ounces semi-sweet or bittersweet chocolate
3 ounces liquid: strong black coffee or Cognac

Melt chocolate and stir in liquid until smooth.

A copper bowl, a whisk and persistence will do the work of the cream of tartar.

APPETIZERS, CHEESES, and PATES

Artichoke with Caper Mayonnaise (Vat and Tonsure)	155
Bagna Cauda (Genoa)	45
Ceviche (Couch Street Fish House)	23
Chilled Oregon Crawfish (Belinda's)	3
Crawfish Appetizers (Jake's)	77
Escargots Bourguignonne (Brasserie Montmartre)	15
Fresh Cream Cheese (Indigine)	71
Hot Artichoke with Hollandaise Sauce (The London Grill)	101
Mousse of Chicken Livers (Pettygrove House)	121
Pâté (L'Auberge)	85
Pâté de Canard aux Pistaches (L'Escargot)	93
Sorbet of Tomato and Orange (Pettygrove House)	122
Sweetbreads Meunière (Belinda's)	6
Top Hats (Henry Thiele's)	55

BEVERAGES

Iced Mint Tea (Old Portland Post Office)	112
Mint Julep (Old Portland Post Office)	111
Spanish Coffee (Huber's)	67

BREADS and BATTERS

Crêpes (Crêpe Faire)	32
Fred's Bread (The Woodstove)	176
Sage Dressing (Huber's)	66
Sopaipillas (Señor Korte Restaurante)	130

DESSERTS and DESSERT ACCENTS

Biscochitos (Señor Korte Restaurante)	133
Boccone Dolce (Genoa)	51
Boccone Dolce (The Woodstove)	180
Bread Pudding (Huber's)	67
Carolyn's Blueberry Pudding with Lemon Wine Sauce (Old Portland Post Office)	117

Cheesecake (Jake's)	81
Chocolate Fondue (Couch Street Fish House)	27
Chocolate Glaze (The Woodstove)	181
Crème Patissière à la Liqueur de Framboise (Belinda's)	11
Filling (Vat and Tonsure)	158
Fresh Ginger Cheesecake (Indigine)	73
Fresh Raspberry Sauce (Eat Your Heart Out)	41
Fresh Raspberry Tart (Belinda's)	10
Frosting (Silver Garden)	143
Ice Cream with Peaches and Sauterne (Winterborne)	169
Lemon Filling (Brasserie Montmartre)	19
Lemon Mousse with Fresh Raspberry Sauce (Eat Your Heart Out)	41
Meringue (The Woodstove)	181
Meringue Gâteau with Strawberries and Crème Chantilly (Pettygrove House)	125
Nusstorte (Silver Garden)	143
Parfait aux Framboises (L'Escargot)	97
Pastry (Vat and Tonsure)	158
Pâte Brisée (Belinda's)	10
Pot de Crème au Chocolat (L'Auberge)	89
Princess Charlotte Pudding (Henry Thiele's)	59
Raspberry Ice (Crêpe Faire)	33
Sour Cream Peach Pie (Vat and Tonsure)	158
Sweet Dough (Brasserie Montmartre)	19
Tarte au Citron (Brasserie Montmartre)	19
Topping (Jake's)	81
Topping (Vat and Tonsure)	159
Whipped Cream with Raspberry Liqueur (Belinda's)	9

ENTREES

Branzino alla Zoni (Genoa)	48
Breast of Duckling with Limes and Sesame (The Woodstove)	177
Camphor Wood and Tea Smoked Duck (Uncle Chen's)	147
Carne Adovada (Señor Korte Restaurante)	132
Carre d'Agneau Montmartre (Brasserie Montmartre)	17
Chicken Mendoza (Silver Garden)	139
Crab Legs Kasseri with Rice (Jake's)	78
Fennel Pork Roast with Fresh Broccoli (Vat and Tonsure)	156

Filleta alla Cacciatora (Genoa)	49
Gâteau of Puréed Vegetables and Chicken Mousseline with Mustard Sauce (Crêpe Faire)	31
General Tso's Chicken (Uncle Chen's)	149
German Pot Roast (Henry Thiele's)	56
Lamb Roast with Dijon Mustard, Herbs and Grand Marnier (The London Grill)	105
Middle East Casserole (Eat Your Heart Out)	38
Moules et Crevettes à la Marinière (L'Auberge)	87
Oyster Pan Roast (Old Portland Post Office)	115
Poulet au Beurre (L'Auberge)	88
Red and White (Couch Street Fish House)	26
Roast Chicken with Bleu Cheese and Shrimp Stuffing (Indigine)	72
Roast Squab with Thyme (Pettygrove House)	124
Roast Turkey with Sage Dressing and Gravy (Huber's)	65
Saumon en Croûte Val de Loire avec Sauce Beurre Bercy (L'Escargot)	95
Scallops in Vermouth (Winterborne)	165
Shanghai-Style Sweet and Pungent Pork (Uncle Chen's)	150
Sliced Beef with Orange Peel in Hot Sauce (Uncle Chen's)	148
Stuffed Sole with Tart White Butter (Winterborne)	166
Suprêmes of Pacific Sole with Leeks and Red Wine Sauce (Pettygrove House)	123
Veal Chops aux Fines Herbes (Belinda's)	8

RICE and PASTA

Fettuccine alla Carbonara (Genoa)	47
Panade (L'Auberge)	86
Rice (Brasserie Montmartre)	16
Rice (Jake's)	79
Rice Pilaf (The Woodstove)	178

SALAD DRESSINGS

Cafe House Dressing (Old Portland Post Office)	113
Fresh Basil Dressing (Belinda's)	9
Jake's Dressing (Jake's)	80

Vinaigrette (Winterborne)	166
Vinaigrette (The Woodstove)	179
Vinaigrette (The London Grill)	104
Vinaigrette with Cumin (Eat Your Heart Out)	40

SALADS

A Light Green Salad (The Woodstove)	179
Cole Slaw (Huber's)	64
Fresh Spinach Salad with Cafe House Dressing (Old Portland Post Office)	113
Greens with Fresh Basil Dressing (Belinda's)	9
Leaf Lettuce Salad with Vinaigrette (Winterborne)	166
London Grill Dinner Salad (The London Grill)	104
Marinated Dungeness Crab Salad (Crêpe Faire)	31
Morrocain Salad (Eat Your Heart Out)	40
Pickled Vegetable Salad (Uncle Chen's)	151
Salad with Jake's Dressing (Jake's)	80
Salade et Brie (Brasserie Montmartre)	18
Tomato Salad (Vat and Tonsure)	157
Watercress, Butter Lettuce, and Shrimp Salad (Couch Street Fish House)	24

SAUCES and SPECIAL SEASONINGS

Béarnaise Sauce (Silver Garden)	141
Brine (Henry Thiele's)	57
Brown Sauce (Henry Thiele's)	57
Brown Veal Stock (The London Grill)	106
Coulis of Crayfish (The Woodstove)	174
Court Bouillon (Belinda's)	7
Curry Sauce (Brasserie Montmartre)	16
Hollandaise Sauce (The London Grill)	102
Madeira Sauce (Silver Garden)	140
Mustard Sauce (Crêpe Faire)	33
Pesto (Genoa)	46
Red Sauce (Winterborne)	164
Sauce Beurre Bercy (L'Escargot)	96

Sauce Rémoulade (Belinda's)	4
Sauce Robert (The London Grill)	106
Spiced Court Bouillon (Belinda's)	3
Tart White Butter (Winterborne)	167
Turkey Gravy (Huber's)	66

SOUPS

Bisque d'Ecrevisses (L'Escargot)	94
Charleston Corn Soup (Old Post Office Cafe)	114
Chilled Cucumber Soup (Eat Your Heart Out)	37
Chilled Spring and Summer Cucumber Soup (The London Grill)	103
Cream of Turkey Soup (Huber's)	63
German Onion Soup (Silver Garden)	138
Mediterranean Fish Soup (Winterborne)	164
Minestrone Verde al Pesto (Genoa)	46
Potage Velouté aux Chanterelles (L'Auberge)	86
Purée of Parsnip Soup (Belinda's)	5
Sorrel and Oyster Soup (Couch Street Fish House)	25
Soup Purée of Leek, Potato, and Carrot (The Woodstove)	177

VEGETABLES and SIDE DISHES

Artichoke with Caper Mayonnaise (Vat and Tonsure)	155
Broccoli (Vat and Tonsure)	157
Carote al Burro e Formaggio (Genoa)	50
Carrots (Brasserie Montmartre)	16
Chef's Vegetables (Silver Garden)	142
Chili Rellenos con Queso (Señor Korte Restaurante)	131
Julienne de Legumes Almandine (L'Escargot)	96
Posole Stew (Señor Korte Restaurante)	129
Potato Pancakes (Henry Thiele's)	58
Silver Garden Ratatouille (Silver Garden)	137
Southern Candied Tomatoes (Old Portland Post Office)	116
Sweetbreads Meunière (Belinda's)	6
Tomatoes Stuffed with Cauliflower Purée (Couch Street Fish House)	27
Vegetables à la Juniper (Winterborne)	168

ABOUT THE AUTHORS

Emily Crumpacker, a native Portlander, has worked as a *stagiaire* (chef's assistant) at Ecole de Cuisine La Varenne in Paris, finishing with La Varenne's Grand Diplome. Emily taught cuisine courses at L'Academie Paris-Americaine before returning to Portland. She now teaches at La Cuisine School of Cooking in Seattle, and also works in Portland, teaching and consulting on food-related subjects.

Muriel Bevilacqua Logan, a seasoned traveler, brings her first-hand knowledge of Arabic, Portuguese, Tunisian and French cuisines to a long-time love of cooking—much enhanced by attendance at four culinary schools in France and several in Seattle. Muriel, currently apprenticing in one of Seattle's finest restaurant kitchens, writes articles and reviews for the monthly publication, *A Gourmet's Notebook*.

A Collection of Gourmet Recipes From the Finest Chefs in the Country!

If you enjoyed Dining In—Portland,
additional volumes are now available:

Please send me the quantity checked:

—Dining In—Monterey Peninsula
—Dining In—San Francisco
—Dining In—Minneapolis/St. Paul
—Dining In—Dallas
—Dining In—Portland

—Dining In—Chicago
—Dining In—Houston
—Dining In—Los Angeles
—Dining In—Seattle

—and available by November 1979:

—Dining In—St. Louis
—Dining In—Toronto

— Dining In—Pittsburgh

TO ORDER, SEND $7.95 PLUS $1.00 POSTAGE AND HANDLING FOR EACH BOOK

ORDER FORM

BILL TO
name _____
address _____
city _____ state ____ zip ____

PAYMENT ENCLOSED   CHARGE TO: Visa # _____ Exp. date ____
Master Chg. # _____ Exp. date ____

Signature _____

SHIP TO
name _____   name _____
address _____   address _____
city _____   city _____
state/zip _____   state/zip _____

Peanut Butter Publishing, Peanut Butter Towers
2733 - 4th Ave. So., Seattle, WA 98134